Know Your People

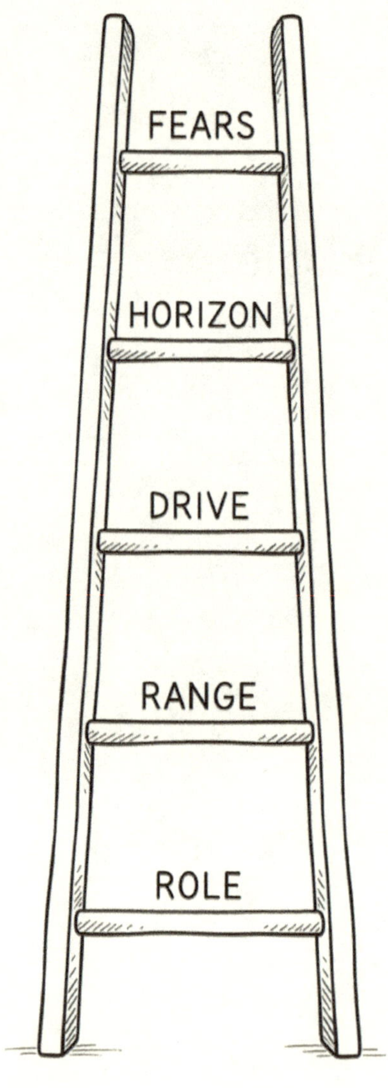

FEARS
HORIZON
DRIVE
RANGE
ROLE

Know Your People

How Great Managers
Earn the Truth
Their People Won't Say

Oz Akan

Ever On Labs

Atlanta, 2026

Published by Ever On Labs, Atlanta

ISBN: 979-8-9961162-0-1

First Edition

Version 0.158

Names and identifying details in personal stories have been changed throughout. Where helpful, dates and locations have been made deliberately vague. The substance of the stories is true.

Contents

Part III: The Team Around the Work

Preface

*"It is impossible for a man to learn
what he thinks he already knows."*

— Epictetus

few weeks into a consulting engagement, I joined the team's weekly meeting. The manager led the whole session, solving each problem as it came up and assigning fixes before moving on. He was deeply technical and seemed to be the strongest engineer in the room. He always called on the same person first. The rest of the team took notes. When one engineer tried to suggest a different design approach, the manager listened for about ten seconds, then said, "I think what we want to do is—" and laid out his own solution. It was reasonable. It also ended the conversation.

After the meeting, the engineer caught up with me in the hallway and explained the approach he had wanted to suggest. It was just as good as the manager's, and probably faster to deliver. I asked why he hadn't said more of that in the meeting. He told me there was no point. Once the manager decided on a direction, that was it. "We'll do it his way. That's how it works here."

I saw this pattern again and again, in different forms. When a team struggled, the manager was usually at the center of it.

Struggling teams were easy to spot. The harder case was the team that looked fine until you knew where to look. The work got done, the team was busy, and the manager looked capable. Still, week after week, something was off. People didn't share ideas out loud. They waited for direction instead of making their own calls. The work kept shipping on time; you had to be in the room to see what wasn't.

After a decade of leading teams, I spent another decade as a principal consultant at AWS. I worked with engineering leaders inside some of the largest companies in the world, on the problems that had needed outside help. The same pattern kept showing up. At the root was the same gap: capable, well-meaning managers who knew the role but not the person. Over time, I started seeing the gap as a five level climb based on how well you know someone, with a different kind of help becoming possible at each level. I call it the Truth Ladder. It is what I wish someone had given me earlier.

This book is that system. It was assembled from years of building teams, making mistakes, reading, and watching what separates the people who grow those around them from the people who don't. Some of it came from books and research. Most came from what I watched happen in teams, over years, as both the manager and the consultant called in for technical problems, only to keep finding people problems underneath.

The stories in this book come from technology, which is the setting I know best. Managers in adjacent fields (product, design, consulting, operations) will recognize most of what is here; I have kept the mechanics specific enough to travel. One example travels further than that list: a retail store manager named Mira appears in one chapter as a thought experiment, testing whether the same mechanics hold where the work and the vocabulary are different.

Whether you've been managing your team for a month or for years, the people across from you are doing the math on what is safe to say, and on whether there is any point. The rest of this book is what to do about it.

In This Chapter

The Trap That Gets Everyone

What This Book Is

The Four Parts

Introduction

> *"The most important thing in communication is hearing what isn't said."*
>
> — Peter Drucker

You were promoted for what you could do. You'll be remembered for what you helped others become.

"He always knew exactly where the project stood."

S MOOTHNESS , in the form of an easy one-on-one or a quick agreement, is not proof of trust. It may be proof of carefulness. A direct report does not talk to a manager the way they talk to a peer. They talk through risk: through the knowledge that your opinion shapes what work they get, how they are evaluated, and what doors open next. Warmth softens that asymmetry — the gradient between someone whose opinion shapes your career and someone whose opinion does not — but it does not remove it.

This is the quiet fact underneath the craft of managing people. You can be warm, capable, and well-intentioned and still spend years hearing the polished version of your team. The person across from you is doing the math, in the second between your question and their answer, on what is safe to say. The work of management is to know them well enough anyway. Well enough to help each person reach clear outcomes. And to remember that being known costs them something too: every honest answer is one they can't take back.

That is the weight of this job. You went from being good at your work to being responsible for other people doing theirs. You probably did it without a manual.[1] Maybe there was a training session. Maybe a few frameworks. But nothing that prepared you for the part where another person sits across from you and you are responsible for what becomes of their work.

The Trap That Gets Everyone

When you get promoted and nobody teaches you the craft, you become busy. Emails, status updates, deliverables, calendars. Somewhere in there, you make a quiet transition nobody warns you about: you stop being a leader of people and become a manager of tasks.

> *The spreadsheet will always feel more urgent than the one-on-one. The product review will always feel more consequential than the career conversation.*

The gravity of busyness pulls you constantly toward managing tasks and away from leading people. The job is to push back on it every week.

What This Book Is

Most management advice fails at the point of use. It is either rigorously researched and inert (frameworks that describe a good manager without telling you what to do on Monday) or it is inspirational language: *be present, be authentic, be vulnerable.* True in the abstract. Useless in the moment when someone is upset about something real.

This book is the missing third thing: an operating system for the human side of management. Most management problems are knowing problems. The power asymmetry between you and a direct report cannot be dissolved, only softened. The work is to lower the cost of truth, climb what you know one level at a time, and use what you learn ethically.

Knowing each person well enough to help them is not a supporting skill of the job. It is the job. Clear outcomes are the floor you stand on to do it: necessary, unimpressive, and not the center of this book.

Most management writing treats the gradient as something warmth and vulnerability can dissolve. It cannot. Forgetting that is how you start exploiting what you learn. Gently, with good intentions, and without noticing.

The Truth Ladder is the instrument for climbing what you know; Chapter 2 is what keeps the climb honest.

The Four Parts

Face the Job is the diagnostic: the gradient that warmth softens but cannot remove, the trust built under it, and the restraint that keeps knowing honest.

Know Your People is the weekly rhythm — one-on-ones, listening, motivation, recognition, career conversations — that deepens what you know about each person.

The Team Around the Work is how what you know reaches the work: clear outcomes, peer trust when you are not in the room, and the same practice scaled when the team grows or applied upward when you manage your own boss.

What You Carry is what the work does to the manager: the weight you hold, what you absorb on the team's behalf, and how to stay accurate while the work goes on.

If you want to start before reading the whole thing, turn the page. The **30-day Quick Start** that follows is one practice per week, starting Monday.

In This Chapter

Quick Start: Your First 30 Days

You don't need to finish this book before you start using it. The four weeks below introduce one practice at a time, in the order that produces the fastest visible change. Each builds on the last. By the end of Week 4, you will have started doing the work this book is about — knowing the people on your team well enough to help them. The outcomes you sharpen along the way are the floor that work stands on.

The chapters that follow give you the reasoning. This page gives you Monday.

Week 1: Restructure Your One-on-Ones

Take your existing one-on-one meetings and apply the five-section structure from Chapter 6:

1. **Accomplishments** (5 min) — What went well this week?
2. **Blocked items** (5–10 min) — Where are you stuck? What do you need from me?
3. **Next week** (5 min) — What are your top priorities? Are we aligned?
4. **Areas to develop** (5 min) — What skill are you working on?
5. **Quarterly goals** (as needed) — Where do we stand?

Tell each person: this meeting is yours. You set the agenda. I'll listen. End every one-on-one with something forward-looking and affirming.

If you don't have regular one-on-ones, start them this week. Weekly, 25 minutes. Protect one-on-ones the way you'd protect a meeting with your own manager: reschedule only when you genuinely must.

Week 2: Notice

For each person on your team, name one specific thing they did this week and why it mattered. Say it to them, in the room or in writing — not banked for a review cycle. This is the recognition direction in the weekly rhythm (Chapter 5); twelve weeks of consistent positive attention can multiply engagement by up to three times. (Chapter 9)

Notice is a habit, not an event. The week you start it is the week the team starts to feel it.

Week 3: Ask the Three Questions

In this week's one-on-ones, ask each person:

1. Where do you feel most constrained?
2. Where do you feel most stretched?
3. What are we building that you actually care about?

These surface what is blocking the energy each person already brings. When an answer comes back thin, you have a diagnosis — usually one you are better positioned to act on than the person living with it. Constraint, fix the permission. Stretch, hand them a problem worth owning. Meaning, put the recipient of the work back in view. (Chapter 8)

Week 4: Run Your First Start, Stop, Continue

Gather your team for 30–45 minutes. Ask three questions:

- **Start:** What should we begin doing that we're not doing today?
- **Stop:** What should we stop doing that isn't working?

- **Continue:** What's working well that we should keep doing?

Collect the answers. Then pick one item from each category and commit to it publicly, with a timeline. Follow through visibly in subsequent meetings.

This week, also pick one handoff on your team that is consistently going wrong — the place where work changes hands and something gets dropped or routed through you instead of between the two people involved. Put the two people in a room and ask them to write down, in their own words, what a good handoff between them looks like. Use the handoff contract template in the toolkit as a prompt. Do not write the contract yourself. This is where peer trust lives or dies. (Chapter 12)

Week 4 closes the loop on weeks 1–3. You've restructured how you meet with people, built a weekly habit of attention, run the diagnostic that surfaces what's actually getting in the way, and named one piece of the work that needs a contract between two people — not a manager in the middle.

The rest of the book is the reasoning behind these practices and the ones you haven't met yet. The toolkit at the back is the field kit.

PART I

Face the Job

What great managers actually do and why most were never taught it. A diagnostic for where you stand today, the gradient that warmth softens but cannot remove, the trust you build daily under that gradient, and the restraint that keeps the knowing honest.

In This Chapter

Outcomes Without Knowing

The Manager Effect

How You Want to Be Treated

Four Patterns

Your First Job as a Manager

The Five Levels

Where Are You Now?

Three Ideas to Carry

The Truth Ladder

1

> *"The task of leadership is not to put greatness into peo-*
> *ple, but to elicit it, for the greatness is there already."*
>
> —John Buchan

Outcomes are the floor every manager stands on. What separates the great ones is how well they know the people doing the work.

"It turns out there was a person behind the job title."

GREAT management means knowing each person on the team well enough to help them achieve outcomes only they can achieve. Outcomes are assumed; without them, no one has a destination. But outcomes do not define the manager. Knowing the people does.

Knowing isn't binary. It moves through five levels, from role to fears, and how far you climb with each person decides what kind of manager you are to them. I call it the Truth Ladder, and it is the spine of this book.

> *Most management problems start as knowing problems.*

Outcomes Without Knowing

Clear outcomes paired with a shallow read of the people ships the work. It also quietly costs you everything else. Your best people save their ambition for elsewhere. Your quiet people stay quiet. Your struggling people keep struggling, because the gap between "hit the target" and "here is what is in the way for you specifically" is exactly where the manager used to sit, and no longer does.

High performers are easy to under-know because their output keeps reassuring you. They deliver on time. They make the right calls. Meetings with them are easy. Nothing forces the relationship deeper. That is the trap. You may know exactly what a strong performer can do. You may have no idea what moves them, or where they want to go next. You may not see what has gone stale, what they have stopped reaching for, or if they are already looking outside the team. None of it shows up in the work.

The pattern repeats. Promoted for delivering results, still delivering results, with the people doing the work as background. When the work piles up, outcomes get your attention and knowing does not, because outcomes are what the job measures you on. Knowing is what the job depends on.

The Manager Effect

Teams in the top quartile of engagement (how invested people feel in their work) outperform those in the bottom in profitability, in sales productivity, and especially in retention.[1] Engaged teams perform better. The reverse does not hold.[2]

Call this the Manager Effect. The manager is the largest single variable in whether a team is engaged, and the most common reason people leave. Half of employees have quit a job to escape one.[3]

Often what people leave is the manager who never knew them. Buckingham and Coffman argued in *First, Break All the Rules* a generation ago that great managers individualize: they treat each report as a different problem rather than applying a uniform practice.[4] This book takes up the next problem. Individualization assumes you can see each person clearly enough to tailor anything. The Truth Ladder is about whether you can. What stands between you and that seeing is power itself. The asymmetry it creates. The trust required to soften it. The restraint that keeps the knowing honest.

How You Want to Be Treated

Every Friday, a few teams gathered for an hour to share wins from the week, celebrate birthdays, and give people a chance to socialize. It wasn't a working meeting. Nathan's attendance had been inconsistent. He would come one week and skip the next. He always had a reason. A task he couldn't step away from. A deadline he was pushing against. I kept inviting him, not as a directive but because I thought he'd enjoy being there. Eventually he started showing up.

One Friday, during the meeting, I acknowledged something he had done that week. Publicly, in front of the team. I thought I was recognizing good work. I watched his face turn red as I spoke, and I kept going, because I read the flush as the good kind of embarrassment, the kind you feel when you're being praised and don't know where to look.

He never came to another team meeting.

For weeks afterward, there was always something. A call he couldn't leave. A blocker that needed his full attention. A reason to step out of the office during exactly the hour we gathered. I had talked him into a room meant for celebration, and once he was there, I had made him the center of attention in front of people from across the org. He never gave me the chance to do it again.

My mistake was reading him through myself. I am not fully comfortable in group settings either, so when I saw his face flush I took it as the same self-conscious reaction I would have had: awkward on the surface, glad underneath. That wasn't what he was feeling. I had treated him the way I would have wanted to be treated, and I didn't know him well enough to see the difference.

That is the golden rule for management. *Treat people the way they need to be treated, not the way you would want to be.* Public praise that feels earned to one person feels exposing to another. A sharp critique that motivates one person demoralizes another. A hands-off approach that reads as trust to a veteran reads as abandonment to someone new.

Four Patterns

You have worked for at least one of these. Probably more than one. Sort managers along two axes — how clearly they tell you what success looks like, and how well they know the person doing the work — and four kinds appear.

The Ghost. You cannot quite tell what they want. They are friendly in meetings, distant in private. Their feedback is positive and vague. Their plans, if there are plans, live somewhere you cannot see them. You write your own job description and hope it matches the version in their head. Months go by. The work is fine. You are not sure whether you are valued or invisible.

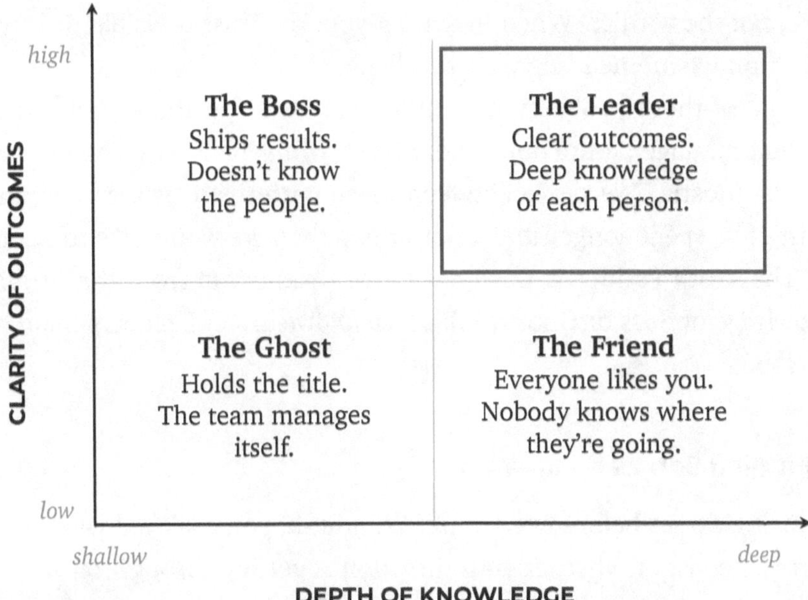

The Boss. They know what needs to happen and they tell you. The work ships. Targets are met. They do not really know you, and you are interchangeable with the person in the next chair, who they also do not really know. You learn fast which version of yourself gets the better assignments, and you start performing it. The strongest people on the team thrive. The rest learn to look like the strongest.

The Friend. They know you. They remember the names of your kids and ask how the move went. The one-on-ones are warm. You like them. You also have no idea where the team is going. Priorities shift slowly. Trade-offs never get named out loud. Your career might be drifting and they are too kind to tell you. You stay because the relationship is real. You leave when you realize the relationship was the only thing the job gave you.

The Leader. They know what the team is for, and they know who you are. The two are connected. The work you get matches what you can do and what you want next. When they correct you, you hear the care, not the verdict. When they trust you, the trust is visible. It is the direction we are heading with this book.

One of those probably made you picture a specific person: your current manager, a previous one, maybe yourself. That recognition is the diagnostic. We move between these patterns over a career, and most of us spend longer in Boss or Friend than we would like to admit.

The Truth Ladder is how you move. You climb from the *surface knowledge* of Boss or Ghost to the *deep knowledge* of Leader, person by person.

Your First Job as a Manager

Knowing comes before everything. Without it, you can't tell what each person needs, or whether your direction is getting through.

Getting there requires them to let you in, and they won't unless they feel safe. Psychological safety (the shared belief that the team is safe for speaking up, disagreeing, and admitting mistakes) is the precondition for candor.[5] Without it, every question you ask gets a polished answer. You learn the performance persona, not the person.

That precondition reframes the job itself. Your first job is to know the people well enough that your direction reaches each of them specifically. The OKRs, the Jira board, the 90-day plan, the "Here's how I like to work" doc. Those come after.

> *The real work of management is knowing the people behind the work.*

The Five Levels

Here are the five rungs of the Truth Ladder. Each unlocks something the rung below it cannot.

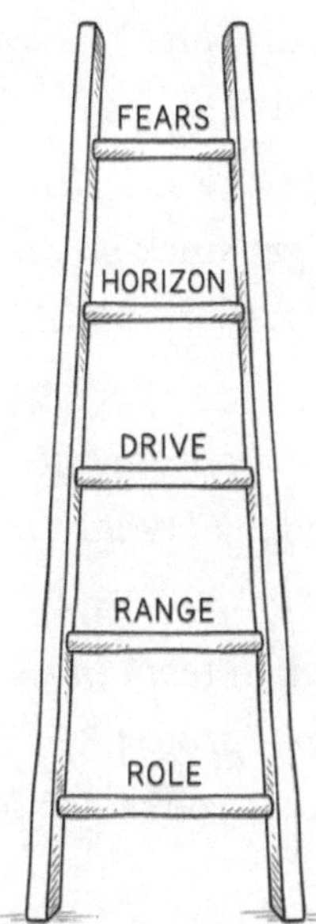

Level 1: Role. What they are responsible for. You know their name, their title, and the scope of work their job names. Every manager starts here. For some relationships, this is the right level.

Level 2: Range. What they finish in a day, and what takes them three. You know their capabilities, where they stretch and where they run out. This lets you give useful feedback and assign the right work.

Level 3: Drive. What moves them. You know what moves them and what drains them. This lets you motivate without guessing and recognize in ways that fit the person.

Level 4: Horizon. Where they want to be in three years, and what stands between here and there. You know what they want next, and what they want after that. This lets you develop their career instead of just managing their output.

Level 5: Fears. What holds them back. You know what's behind it: the doubt, the past experience, the unspoken constraint. This lets you coach through what matters most.

Managers use different vocabulary at each level.

- **Level 1.** *"What's on your plate this week?" / "Can you take the migration?"* Task assignment.
- **Level 2.** *"Your write-ups are the clearest on the team. Lead the external comms." / "You get stuck on naming decisions. Let me pair you with someone who's faster on that."* Matching work to known range.
- **Level 3.** *"The last three onboarding docs came from you. You come alive when you're teaching." / "What's in your week that you would pay to avoid?"* Naming what moves them and what drains them.
- **Level 4.** *"You want to lead a team in two years. The gap is breadth. Let's find a cross-functional project." / "What would you want to be working on in five years that you're not doing today?"* The horizon is years, not sprints.
- **Level 5.** *"The last time you pushed back in that meeting, you went quiet for two days. What happened?" / "You haven't put your hand up for the last two promotion rounds. Is there something in your head that says you shouldn't?"* Naming what is in the way without making it a performance issue.

If most of your conversations with someone stay in the first two rows, that is where you are on the Ladder with them.

You don't reach Level 5 by asking direct questions in week one. You earn it through months of trust, listening, and consistent follow-through. It happens when you notice that your engineer goes quiet in large meetings but lights up when paired with one other person. It happens when you realize your product manager gives their best work after a deadline, not before. It happens when you learn that your designer's reluctance to push back is fear of conflict, rooted in a previous manager who punished dissent. That last one is Level 5.

Why go deeper? Engagement scores improve, and that alone would justify the work. But the bigger change happens inside the other person.

The work is harder than it sounds. The moment one person can affect another's job — what they work on, how they're evaluated, what door opens next — the power gradient between them shapes what gets said. People spend enormous energy at work protecting themselves. They manage impressions. They hide gaps. They filter what they say to match what they think you want to hear. That energy isn't going into the work. A manager who knows someone at Level 1 gets the performance persona. Climbing the Ladder is how you get past it. A manager who reaches Level 3 or 4 starts to dissolve the need for the performance. The person stops rehearsing and starts thinking, because someone has finally seen them clearly enough that the rehearsal is no longer necessary.

When you know someone well enough, you become a mirror. You notice strengths they undervalue, fears they have not named, aspirations they have not admitted to themselves. You reflect those things back, and the person sees something in that reflection they could not see on their own. The Truth Ladder is a tool for the other person, not a checklist for the manager.

Nathan's story was projection. Reading someone through yourself. The opposite mistake is reading the surface and stopping there.

I almost did exactly that with someone on my own team. Early in a new role, I inherited a team member who seemed to be struggling. He stayed late most nights, appeared constantly busy, but his output didn't match the hours. Tasks that his peers finished in a day took him three. I read it as knowledge gaps and weak problem-solving. Maybe he wasn't cut out for the work.

I was wrong.

It took weeks of working alongside him before I saw what I had been missing. He was terrified of making a mistake. He would reach a decision point and freeze, cycling through options, second-guessing each one, unable to commit because every path carried the risk of looking foolish. The same fear kept him from asking the questions that would have taught him. The knowledge gaps were real, but fear was the bottleneck.

Once I understood that, everything about how I managed him changed. I coached him to take small, recoverable risks and paired him with a senior teammate so he could see what "good enough to ship" looked like from someone other than his manager. The paralysis loosened. The quality of his work improved, because he was spending his energy solving problems instead of second-guessing himself.

I had been assuming fairness meant uniformity. He needed me closer, for a specific reason and a limited time.

Closeness like that has to be earned. The Ladder moves at the person's pace; you can only climb as far as they have invited you.

It also bounds from your side. With eight reports and a crisis, you won't reach Level 4 with all of them. If your own boss is absent or you're burned out, you won't either. There is a limit to what you can do, no matter how much you care.

The Ladder can also harm the person it claims to serve. Pressed too soon, mistaken for a license to keep asking, used to steer rather than help. Chapter 4 develops the full ethics.

Information that makes you a better manager *for that person* is what you are going after. Information that makes you more useful to yourself is the trap.

Knowing each person is where the work starts.

Your instinct will be to call it managing performance, when what you are managing is your picture of the person.

Where Are You Now?

Before you read further, sit with these four questions. Answer each one honestly. There is no score. The ones that give you pause are where to start.

1. Can I name what specifically motivates each person on my team?

2. Do I know where each person wants to be in two or three years?

3. In my one-on-ones, how much of the talking do I do (closer to 10% or 50%)?

4. Does each person on my team experience recognition differently, and do I adjust for that?

A companion self-check, using the practices the next chapters introduce, sits in the toolkit's Manager Self-Assessment.

Three Ideas to Carry

- **Knowing is the job. Outcomes are the floor.** Outcomes ship the work. Knowing decides whether the work reaches the people you're responsible for, and whether the problems you end up dealing with are the ones you saw coming or the ones you didn't.

- **Treat each person the way *they* need to be treated.** The golden rule, applied to management, has you managing your own preferences through someone else. Range, drive, horizon, and fear are different on each side of the desk. The work is to stop assuming otherwise.

- **Most managers stop at Level 2.** The performance persona is what the asymmetry of the relationship gives you for free. Climbing past it is how you reach the actual person whose work you're responsible for.

In This Chapter

2

Power Bends What You Hear

> *"Attention is the rarest and purest form of generosity."*
>
> — Simone Weil

Warmth softens the gradient between you and a report. It does not erase it.

'Let me know if anything ever feels off.'

Aɴ engineer joined our team in the fall. He had come from a smaller company where he had been one of the more senior people on a small team, and now he was one of the more junior people in a larger one. In his first weeks he was thoughtful in meetings, warm with his peers, quick to volunteer. In our one-on-ones he told me the work was good, the team was good, he was learning a lot.

I asked more than once whether anything was unclear, whether he needed anything from me. He said no every time. I believed him. Nothing about it felt difficult, and I took that as a good sign.

About two months in, a deadline slipped. A day, then two days, then most of a week. When we sat down to talk about it, I was expecting a normal project conversation. A bad estimate. A missing dependency.

After a long pause, he told me he had been unsure of what was being asked of him for most of the project, and had not felt he could say so. He had hoped the scope would clarify itself. Then he had hoped the senior engineers around him would clarify it for him. Then he had started building what he thought was roughly the right thing, hoping he could correct course if he was wrong.

I asked why he had not come to me. He told me, after a longer pause, that he had been afraid of something he had trouble naming. He thought I would start to revise my picture of him. If he asked too many basic questions early, I might quietly decide he was not as strong as I had thought when I hired him. He thought he could hold the picture in place by looking steady until he had caught up.

If he had come to me with questions, it wouldn't have even crossed my mind to revise my picture of him. I would have helped him from week one. The fear that I might was enough to keep him silent.

> *He was not afraid of me. He was afraid of the picture I would form if he asked.*

The Ladder Bends Under Power

The Truth Ladder in Chapter 1 described five levels of knowing a person. Role, range, drive, horizon, fears. The practices in this book build that knowing with the understanding that power bends the climb.

A manager is not a neutral presence in a report's working life. You decide what work they get, how they are evaluated, and in many organizations what doors open next. Your people know that. Even when they like you and trust your intentions, they route what they say to you through the fact that your opinion can affect their future.

This is not a failure of the relationship. It is the structure of it.

The mistake is to assume good intentions have erased the asymmetry. They have not; they soften it without removing it. A direct report does not talk to their manager the way they talk to a peer. They talk through risk.

I call this the gradient. It is the power asymmetry between a manager and a direct report, and what that asymmetry does to honesty.

A gradient is a slope, not a switch. It varies in steepness. It is gentle with a tenured employee who has options and steep under a PIP, a layoff threat, or a job that someone's right to stay in the country depends on. It always points one direction. Power flows downhill from the manager to the report, and honesty has to climb against it. That is the gradient. You can soften it. You cannot remove it as long as the two positions differ. And it is structural, not moral: a property of the terrain you both stand on, not a verdict on either of you. Reading it honestly is the work; pretending it is flat is the mistake.

Once you see the gradient, the engineer's "no" stops being a puzzle. He was not withholding. Silence cost him less than questions would have. A few things get easier from there. You stop reading agreement as honesty. You stop treating a quiet one-on-one as evidence that nothing is being held back. You stop thinking of the Ladder as something to complete. You start thinking of it as something you earn, one rung at a time, while the other person decides whether the cost of the next rung is worth paying.

What Power Distorts

Power slows down disclosure. It also changes the answers you get.

Your reports nod before they finish thinking, because disagreement is expensive. They keep a concern quiet when it is not yet serious enough to justify the cost of raising it. And by the time it reaches you, the problem is larger than it needed to be. Your direct questions come back in approved language. The respectable answer about motivation. The promotable answer about ambition. What they leave out is usually more specific. They want stability after a bad year, flexibility for a family thing, the chance to do excellent work without being pushed toward leadership.

None of this is dishonest. It is the price the report has decided to pay for the relationship.

From above, the relationship can look clean: alignment, openness, low drama. From below, it can feel expensive. The question to ask yourself is not whether the relationship is easy. It is whether it is easy because it is safe, or easy because the other person is being careful.

False Signals of Trust

Managers misread several things as closeness. Each is worth naming, because once named they are easier to catch.

Quick agreement is not trust. It is often the fastest exit from a conversation with someone whose opinion carries weight. When a report agrees before you have finished the sentence, they may be ending the risk.

Warmth doesn't promise candor. A report can be friendly with you every week and never tell you anything that would cost them. You will not feel the gap until the work surfaces it.

A difficult story about a weekend is one of the cheaper disclosures. The ones that would actually cost them come much later, if at all: doubts about the work or plans they haven't told you about.

A grateful report is often a guarded one, because gratitude presumes there is something to lose.

Silence at the end of a plan often reads as alignment. It is usually the cost of dissent priced and refused.

The person who asks no questions has usually decided the questions cost too much.

Polished articulacy is the one that fools the most managers. An engineer on my team sounded like the textbook strong employee. She was fluent in our language. She named the growth areas I would have named for her. Her self-assessments mirrored my feedback word for word. For most of a year I believed I knew her well. Then a peer mentioned, in passing, she had been sharply disagreeing with one of my decisions for weeks. None of it came to me. She had learned, somewhere before me, that the efficient way to be trusted by a manager was to sound like someone a manager would already trust. I had been reading the absence of friction as honesty, and receiving the performance as the person.

That kind of smoothness can mean the relationship has earned its ease. It can also mean the other person has decided the cost of truth here is too high. The two can look nearly identical from where you sit, and feel nothing alike from where they do.

Where the Ladder Bends Most

The Ladder bends unevenly under power. Three rungs deserve specific attention.

Level 2, range, is distorted by evaluation anxiety. Most people know their gaps better than they say them. They know what takes too long, what they avoid, what kind of work makes them feel exposed. The question is whether saying those things aloud feels like a path to help or a path to a smaller future. When the relationship is not safe enough, people offer cleaner weaknesses, the ones they can survive professionally. A manager who only hears those can mistake self-protection for self-awareness. Making it safe to say "*I am not good at this yet*" is the first real act of building Level 2.

Level 4, horizon, is vulnerable to prestige. Ask someone where they want to be in three years and many will tell you what they think a strong employee is supposed to want. What they may not say is that they want more breathing room and less stress. Or deeper craft over broader scope. Or a role that fits their life better. All of those are real. In most organizations only some of them feel sayable. If you want the real Level 4, you have to make the non-status answers feel legitimate, and you have to keep making room for them until the person believes you.

Level 5, fears, is where power matters most. A fear spoken to a manager is a fear placed into a relationship that can affect opportunities, evaluations, and the story that gets told about someone's performance. That is why Level 5 is easy to mishandle. The first mistake is asking too directly, too early. "*What are you afraid of?*" is rarely a good management question. It asks for too much before the relationship has earned it. The second mistake is over-interpreting what you infer. Hesitation around conflict, a freeze at decision points, an aversion to visibility, a strong reaction to feedback may all point to a fear. They do not give you the right to name it on someone's behalf. At this level, humility is more useful than cleverness. Sometimes the right move is not to name the fear at all, but to reduce its power in the way you manage around it.

What Steepens the Asymmetry

The gradient is not the same in every relationship. A long-tenured employee with options lives in a different gradient from a new hire still proving they belong. A PIP steepens it. Layoffs and reorganizations steepen it for everyone at once. So does a job someone's right to stay in the country depends on. Someone coming from a punitive workplace may still be reacting to an old manager while sitting across from a better one. Under any of these conditions, honesty costs more.

Instead of asking why a person is not more open with you, ask what makes openness costly here. Often the answer is something you can adjust.

What Raises the Cost of Truth

Before you can lower the cost of truth, you have to see what you are doing that raises it. Most of the common ones are small, well-meant, and invisible to the person doing them. The cost accumulates slowly, as the report quietly learns what is safe to bring you and what is not.

Interrupting. When a report is halfway through naming something uncomfortable, you'll be tempted to finish the sentence for them, to show you have already understood. That closes the door they were about to walk through.

Answering the question you wish they had asked. The report brings a half-formed concern. You respond to a cleaner, more tractable version of it. They learn that half-formed thoughts do not survive the conversation, so they stop bringing them.

Turning uncertainty into a competence judgment. A report says, *"I am not sure how to do this."* You hear weakness. Your face or your tone shows it, briefly. You recover. They do not say that sentence to you again.

Remembering the mistakes longer than the candor. A report comes to you with a miscall on their own. You thank them for the candor. Three months later you reference it in a performance conversation as an example of something they own. The next time, they think harder before bringing you anything unflattering. You have taught them that candor has a memory attached.

Treating dissent as a tone problem. A report pushes back on a decision. Rather than arguing the substance, you note how it came across. You talk about delivery. You have now made the price of disagreement a conversation about them, not about the decision.

Reusing someone's vulnerability. A report told you something hard in confidence. Later, in a meeting where they were present, you used it as context, lightly, even sympathetically. They heard it. They will not bring you that kind of thing again.

None of these needs to be cruel to be costly. They can be small, considered, or done while trying to help. The problem is that each one teaches. Over months, the report adjusts what they bring you, and you end up with the version of them that survived the cost.

Before your next one-on-one, a short self-check.

1. **Interrupted.** Did I finish their sentence when it got uncomfortable?
2. **Wish-question.** Did I answer a cleaner version of what they actually asked?
3. **Competence tell.** Did my face or tone revise their confidence when they named a gap?
4. **Long memory.** Did I reference an old mistake they had already owned to me?
5. **Tone pivot.** Did I respond to their dissent by coaching the delivery?
6. **Reused vulnerability.** Did I use something they told me in confidence as context in another room?

What to Do Differently

The first move is to lower the cost of truth. Say the things that make honest answers safer. *"You do not need a polished answer here." "I would rather hear this rough than hear a cleaner version later." "This will not come back at you later."* Small sentences, said early, said often. They are only as credible as the behavior that follows them. If you react poorly to roughness, no sentence will save you.

The second is to ask less invasive questions. *"What would make this role work better for you?"* goes further than *"What are you afraid of?"*

"*What part of this is heavier than it looks?*" goes further than "*What is stressing you out?*" People will gesture at a fear before they will name it.

The third is to watch behavior more than declarations. The engineer who agrees to the plan in the meeting and spends the next three days working around it. The new hire who says she is fine and starts arriving earlier and leaving later every week. The report who is relaxed with peers and rigid in one-on-ones. The behavior often tells you what the person is not ready to say.

The fourth is to normalize boundaries. Say out loud that people are not expected to disclose more than what helps the work and their own support. If a report believes the bar for a good working relationship is unlimited transparency, they will perform transparency.

The fifth is to treat volunteered vulnerability carefully. When someone opens a door, your instinct will be to walk through it, to prove you were worth the risk, to carry it forward. Resist most of that. Do not retell the story. Do not make it a touchstone in later conversations without their signal. People stop disclosing to a manager who treats every door opened as an invitation to walk through it.

The sixth is to leave two seconds of silence after something uncomfortable. The urge to finish the sentence is what closes the door.

The seventh is to respond to the substance of a pushback, not to its delivery. If the tone also needs a coaching conversation, hold it until a different day and say plainly that it is a separate conversation. The two can both be useful, but combined into one, they teach the report that pushing back was the mistake.

The Report's Calculation

All of that is what you do. The other side of the table is doing its own work.

Every one-on-one starts with a calculation. It happens in the second between the question and the answer. *What is this question really for?*

Which version of the answer keeps me safe? How far can I push the truth without paying for it later?

From your point of view, you get an honest answer.

The report has been doing this math since the interview. By the time they sit across from you, they have built a running model from small data: how you handled the last person who escalated bad news, whether something disclosed in a one-on-one came back in a different room, what happened to a colleague who said something similar in a recent team meeting. The cost of the wrong output was priced in before the question was asked.

It is not hard to imagine being on the report's side of this math. You are sitting in a one-on-one where the honest thing to say is that the project is underwater, the team is behind, exhausted. What comes out of you is a crisper, more composed summary of the same facts. The summary is true. It is also optimized. You leave the meeting slightly lighter, with the quiet knowledge that you bought the lightness with precision. You said the thing you could afford to say.

A report who is careful is one whose reading of the room told them that careful was the right price. Sometimes the reading is wrong. Sometimes the previous manager was bad and you are inheriting the carefulness. Sometimes the reading is correct, and you are the last one to know.

The signals a report is reading are mostly small. A body that shifted when the last difficult thing was disclosed. A one-on-one that felt like it was being run through a cooler filter. A remembered disclosure that came back as leverage instead of care. A small correction in a team meeting that everyone felt. Reports read every one of these signals without anyone naming them.

Smoothness is not proof of trust was the view from above. The view from below is its inversion: *carefulness is not the absence of trust. It is what trust has cost so far.* When a report gets a little less careful each time, they are watching you and revising the price. Your job is to keep behaving in ways that let the price fall.

How to Tell Whether Truth Is Actually Safe

The easiest way to deceive yourself about a working relationship is to ask, generally, whether it feels good. A different set of questions is more useful.

Do your reports revise your thinking, or do they mostly receive it? A relationship in which you give and they nod is cheaper than it looks. A healthier one has traffic going the other way: small corrections, alternative framings, the occasional "*I do not think that is what is going on.*" If the road only runs one direction, you are being agreed with, not understood.

Do they bring you half-formed problems, or only polished updates? Clean updates are pleasant to receive and not very informative. When every one of your reports hands you a clean package, the messy part of the work is happening somewhere you cannot see it.

Do they ever tell you your framing is wrong? Not in a charged way, just as a working correction. "*I don't think that is the bottleneck.*" "*I read that project differently.*" When a team stops challenging the manager, that is silence rather than alignment.

Do they ask for help before the miss, or only after? The point at which help gets asked for is a measurement of the relationship, not of the employee. If the pattern is that you find out about problems once they have slipped, the cost of asking earlier is higher than you think it is.

Do they set boundaries without a long justification? "*I cannot take this on this quarter*" said plainly is a sign of safety. The same sentence braced with three paragraphs of explanation, or offered with an apology, is a sign that the report is preparing for your reaction.

Do they disagree in the room, or only afterwards? If the pushback only ever shows up in one-on-ones, or in writing the next morning, your meetings are optimizing for something other than the best answer. The public version is the filtered one.

None of these is a single measurement. They get easier to answer honestly when you already suspect the answer. Ask the questions anyway. Then notice what you want the answer to be.

When the Problem Is Not a Conversation

Some things do not get solved by asking better. Compensation insecurity. Immigration uncertainty. Mental health. A family in crisis. The aftermath of a prior manager who made honesty unsafe. These situations are not closed by a good one-on-one. They are changed, when they can be changed, by conditions.

Safer deadlines when the person is carrying something heavy at home. A written confirmation when the visa timeline is tight. A clear signal that the performance clock is not running during a medical absence. A short conversation at the end of the week where you tell them, plainly, that the plan is not going to change on them next week.

You do not always need the person to name the pressure before you can reduce it. The signals that something is working will be quieter than the signals that something is wrong.

What Trust Looks Like Here

Trust under power shows up in quiet places. A report escalates a problem earlier than you would have caught it on your own. A self-assessment names a gap the review cycle had not yet surfaced. A disagreement continues past the meeting, coming back in writing the next morning, and the person does not seem worried that the persistence will cost them. Someone says *"I do not know"* in front of people who might have preferred to hear confidence.

Those signals are what trust looks like when the gradient is steep. They look less like closeness and more like work. And they tell you more.

Reading the gradient honestly is the first half of the work. What you do with what you read is the second half. The trust built in ordinary moments is what keeps the careful version of a person from being the only version you ever see.

Three Ideas to Carry

- **Smoothness is not proof of trust.** From above, the relationship looks clean. From below, it can feel expensive. The reports who are most careful with you are usually telling you the most about the gradient between you.

- **False signals look like closeness.** Quick agreement, warmth, a hard story, gratitude, polished articulacy. Each can read as truth and is usually something else. Track them as data, not as proof of where you stand.

- **Carefulness is what trust has cost so far.** When a report becomes less careful with you over time, the price has come down. When they become more careful, you raised it.

In This Chapter

What Predictability Buys

Tell the Truth Early, and Match It With Action

When Trust Is Performed, Not Built

Make It Safe to Disagree

Correct Without Humiliation

After You Break Trust

The Practical Test

Three Ideas to Carry

Trust Before Truth

3

Trust is built or broken in moments managers barely notice.

'The team was in complete agreement, as usual.'

A new senior manager joined our organization. The announcement had come by email a few days earlier: name, title, background. At the townhall where leadership introduced him, he did not open with his credentials or his vision for the team. He talked about his ankles hurting from years of tennis and how he had been trying to find a replacement sport without success. He talked about how it was different when he was younger. The ambitions he had. What drove him then. He mentioned his family, what motivates him at this stage of his life.

I exhaled. He was going to be fine. He was down to earth, thoughtful, someone who reflected on his own experience rather than projecting success. Five minutes earlier I had been bracing for the worst. Now I wanted to walk up and shake his hand, because he had let us see who he was. The higher people climb, the more pressure they feel to appear perfect. He had chosen to show up as a person instead.

I could have been wrong. He might have been performing the warmly self-disclosing version of himself for the audience. Over the next year, my own time with him, and what I heard from people closer to him, told me it had not been performance.

What shifted in that room was not affection. It was price. People were making a fast calculation: if this leader can name something ordinary and imperfect about himself without turning it into theater, maybe the rest of us will not have to perform perfection either. That is what trust does under power. It does not make truth free. It makes truth less expensive.

One story. Five minutes. It did not replace the trust that gets built over months, but it set the tone, and with a new leader, that is often all you have to go on. *The leader goes first*[1]: in vulnerability, in honesty, in self-correction. If the highest-status person in the room cannot acknowledge an ordinary human fact about themselves, nobody else will take the risk.

Trust is what lowers the price of honesty under power. We named the asymmetry in Chapter 2. This chapter is about the daily moves that lower its price. Without that kind of trust, nothing past role is reachable.

What people are tracking, day by day, is predictability under power. Three judgments make up most of trust, and your reports make all three about you whether you intend them or not. Ability, benevolence, integrity.[2] In plain English, *can you do your job? Do you care about me? Do your words match your actions?* Under the gradient, the third one carries the most weight. Ability is read mostly through the work. Benevolence is easy to fake for an hour. Integrity is the one a report can only verify across weeks and it is the one they need most before they will tell you anything that costs them.

So the trust question a report is actually asking is not abstract. *Can I challenge an idea in a meeting without spending the next two weeks wondering whether I damaged our relationship?* The answer is not given by what you say in the moment. It is given by what you have done last time, and the time before that.

What Predictability Buys

Julian joined our team as a project manager. He was organized, responsive, and good with people. But he was suffocating his teammates. Too many check-ins, too many questions, too much involvement in details that were not his to manage. The team could not breathe. From the outside it looked like someone who did not understand boundaries.

By then Julian and I had weeks of one-on-ones behind us, and we had worked through a couple of difficult situations together. That shared ground was what let me finally ask what was really driving the intensity. He told me about a project at his previous company where he had trusted the team and stepped back. People did not show ownership. The project fell apart and he carried the blame. He was not controlling this team because he thought they were weak. He was controlling them because last time something had slipped past him, he had paid for it, and he was not going to fail this one.

Once I heard that, I stopped seeing an overbearing PM and started seeing a person. I helped him understand that ownership ran deep in our culture, that this team was different from the one that had failed him. I talked to the team and asked them to be more visible with their updates for a while, so he could see the ownership in action rather than take it on faith. He eased up. The team started performing the way they could.

Without that conversation, I would have given him feedback about his behavior. With it, I could address the fear underneath. You cannot coach someone through a fear you do not know about. And they will not tell you about it unless trust is already there.

The Julian conversation did not happen because I asked a sharp question. It happened because of the weeks before it. The small commitments kept, the disagreements heard without irritation, the disclosures left where he had put them. None of that looked like trust-building at the time. It looked like an ordinary working relationship. That was the work. The disclosure is what trust earns. The disciplines below are what trust costs.

Tell the Truth Early, and Match It With Action

Most of what breaks trust in ordinary management happens in the gap between what you say and what you do, or between what you know and what you tell. Two disciplines hold that gap closed.

Tell the truth early

Managers delay the truth constantly, usually for reasons that feel noble. They do not want to create anxiety. They want more information first. They hope the issue will resolve itself. Usually they are protecting themselves. When people discover you knew more than you said, or knew earlier than you admitted, they do not experience that as care. They experience it as a breach. What they don't hear from you, they hear from each other, and the version that travels is rarely the whole story.

The asymmetry matters here. When a manager withholds difficult information, the report does not experience the silence as empty. They fill it. They read calendar changes, tone shifts, skipped details, and hallway fragments. The more power you hold over their future, the less silence feels like silence. It feels like information without a frame.

Being vague when the truth is available but difficult is avoidance.

I learned this on a project early in my consulting career. We had identified a serious risk to the engagement, and the team was in the middle of working through it. We were brainstorming options, stress-testing scenarios, debating what could go sideways. None of it was settled. The next day, the customer approached me with questions they should not have had. Someone on the team had shared our internal discussion during a quick sync, not with bad intent, but without the context that would have made the conversation useful. The customer heard what we thought could fail and what we wanted to avoid, but not the reasoning behind any of it. Trust in the team dropped overnight.

The problem was not the information. The problem was that it traveled without its frame. Transparency without judgment — without deciding what is ready to share and what still needs work — is noise, not honesty. Noise, once it reaches a customer, is almost impossible to walk back. The danger runs in both directions. Sharing without judgment destroys trust from one side. Withholding destroys it from the other. Don't hide behind euphemism. Don't say "*some opportunities for improvement*" when you mean performance is not meeting the bar. Say *reorganization* when the plan is a reorganization.

Vague and late: "There may be some changes coming. We'll keep you posted."

Direct and early: "The team is being reorganized. I don't have all the details yet, but here's what I know, and I'll share more as soon as I can."

Match words with actions

Telling the truth is half of integrity. The other half is doing what you said you would do. When a manager's actions drift from their words, trust falls and performance drops with it.[3]

Most trust failures are mundane. Broken small promises like *I'll get back to you by Friday. I will join that meeting. I want you to challenge me if you disagree.* Keep enough of them and trust compounds. Break enough of them and no speech about culture will save you.

The discipline is to make fewer promises, make them more carefully, and treat follow-through as a leadership skill rather than an administrative detail. Before you close your laptop on Friday, go over every commitment you made that week. The "*I'll get back to you,*" the "*I'll think about it,*" the "*I'll look into that.*" Anything unclosed gets a calendar block for the next week. The list is usually shorter than it feels. The ones you forget are the ones that would have cost you most.

One more practice sits alongside the Friday close. Where the Friday close builds integrity (matching words to actions), this one builds benevolence (signaling care). Once a week, scan the team and ask who you have not heard from in a meaningful way since the same time last week. Not the standup check-in. A real exchange. The person who gives you the least bandwidth is rarely the person who needs the least from you. Usually they are the one whose signals you are missing by default. Pick one, and do not let the week close with silence between you.

When Trust Is Performed, Not Built

A few common patterns look like trust and do the opposite work.

Warmth without follow-through. The manager is kind in one-on-ones, remembers birthdays, asks about families. Then the commitment made in one of those meetings does not get kept, and the team learns that warmth doesn't buy action.

Vulnerability staged for credibility. The manager tells a hard story at the all-hands, admits a mistake in a team meeting. Then in a one-on-one where admitting a miss would actually cost them, the manager goes silent. For the team, weeks of behavior weigh more than one practiced story.

"Open door" paired with punitive memory. The manager tells the team to bring anything, push back any time. A report takes the invitation and surfaces something uncomfortable. Weeks later, in a performance conversation, the dissent returns as a data point about their attitude. The team does not confuse that pattern for safety again.

The common thread is memory. Trust is the memory of what you did last time.

Make It Safe to Disagree

Many teams look calm on the surface because disagreement has been trained out of them. People nod in meetings and express their real views in side conversations. That looks like alignment; what it is, is self-protection.

If you want trust, make disagreement normal. Start with the questions you ask. *"Does anyone have concerns?"* is weak. It invites minimal dissent and lets silence masquerade as agreement. Better questions are specific and demanding. *What are we missing? What would make this fail? If you had to argue against this plan, what would you say? Who sees this differently?* What you do after someone answers matters more than the question itself. React to a concern with visible irritation, and you teach the team the cost of speaking up.

The first disagreement after a decision is a test. The report is testing you as much as the idea. Whether you get smaller. Whether you remember the dissent later. Whether you convert the substance into a tone problem. People learn from that first test faster than they learn from any speech about candor.

Correct Without Humiliation

People lose trust in managers who let obvious problems slide just as surely as they lose trust in managers who correct people harshly. In the first case, the team concludes that standards are not real. In the second, they conclude that honesty is unsafe.

The balance is to be direct without being demeaning. Correct the work clearly. Name the behavior specifically. Explain the impact. Stay focused on the issue rather than the person's worth. When a manager says, *"This draft is not yet at the level we need, and I want to help you get it there,"* trust can actually increase. The employee learns two things at once. The bar is real. I will not be humiliated for missing it. People only reach for more when falling short feels survivable.

The same principle holds in the small moments, the ones that do not wait for a one-on-one or a review. Save them up and the feedback gets heavier every day. By the time you deliver it, it sounds like a verdict instead of a conversation. The toolkit's *Feedback in the Moment* card has the three-move structure — what you saw, what it did, what you are curious about — and the conditions it depends on.

Feedback also goes both ways. The manager who gives direct feedback but cannot receive it has built a one-way mirror, and people figure that out fast. The receiving discipline is the same one in Chapter 7. Hear it, do not defend it, summarize back. Under the gradient, this is the rarer half of the practice and the one your team is reading you on.

The hardest version is the performance conversation. This is when the truth is about someone's overall pace or quality, not a single moment. The test for whether you have waited too long is whether the employee looks genuinely surprised when you raise it. A person receiving clear, consistent feedback may disagree with the assessment; they should not be shocked by it. If they are, the signal is about you, not them. The fuller version of that conversation lives inside the one-on-one (see Chapter 6).

After You Break Trust

Managers break trust too. What you do after matters more than the breach itself. You cancel a one-on-one you promised would never get cancelled. You take credit in a meeting for work someone on your team did. You react defensively to feedback you asked for. You say something in frustration that you cannot take back. Your instinct will be to move past it quickly and hope the person forgets. They will remember exactly how it felt, and they will quietly adjust how much of themselves they bring to work.

Recovery has three moves, and they must come in order. Acknowledge it. Specifically, unprompted, without defensiveness. *"I told you I would advocate for that promotion and I didn't follow through. That was my failure."*[4] Leave space for them to react. If you don't, the apology sounds like it was for you, not them. Then change the behavior, because an apology not followed by different behavior is just a preview of the next apology.

Recovered trust can be stronger than trust that was never tested, since people are more likely to share their fears with someone whose relationship has visibly survived damage.

The Practical Test

If you want to know whether you are building trust, do not ask whether your team seems friendly. Ask harder questions. Do people bring me problems early or late? Do they disagree with me in the room or only after? Those are better measures than whether people laugh at your jokes. The disclosure Julian eventually made was downstream of both, asked and answered honestly across the months that came before.

Three Ideas to Carry

- **Trust is what you did last time, not what you said this time.** Memory is the substrate. The team is reading the pattern across months, not the sentence in front of them.
- **Tell the truth early, and match it with action.** The gap between what you say and what you do is where most trust quietly breaks. People do not need you to be right; they need you to be the same person from one week to the next.
- **Recovered trust can be stronger than trust that was never tested.** Acknowledge specifically and unprompted, leave space for the reaction, then change the behavior. People are more likely to share their fears with someone whose relationship has visibly survived damage.

The Ethics of Knowing

4

"The first duty of love is to listen."

— Paul Tillich

You don't climb for a trophy. Ask who the next rung is for before you climb it.

THE Truth Ladder is a tool. Like any tool, it can be used for the person on the other end of it or for yourself, and the line between the two is easier to cross than it looks. The last three chapters were about what makes the climb possible. The Ladder itself, the gradient that complicates it, the trust that lowers the cost of truth. This chapter is about what restraint looks like once the access is real.

The Ladder can harm the person it claims to serve. Pressed too soon, mistaken for a license to keep asking, used to steer rather than to help. Restraint is part of knowing. It is what keeps a manager from turning what she has been told into leverage she did not ask for.

When the Next Rung Isn't Available

Consider an engineer whose work visa is sponsored by her employer. She is excellent, and in her first month she tells her manager, lightly and more than once, that she is grateful to be on the team and will

"

do whatever is needed. Her manager likes her and takes it at face value. He runs the three questions from Chapter 6 (where do you feel most constrained, where most stretched, what are we building that you actually care about) and gets good answers. Clean, considered, respectful of the work. He thinks he has reached Level 3.

He has the polished version.

Not because she is being dishonest. The cost of a rough answer is different for her than for her teammates. If she says a project is draining her, reassignment inside a visa sponsorship is a conversation that travels back to an immigration lawyer. None of those conversations are impossible. They are always more expensive. So she gives the version of herself that is safe to give to a manager whose opinion can affect her petition.

A careful manager figures this out from behavior, not from what she says. She is always at her desk. But she cancels most of the optional ones. The team dinners, the stretch projects that would be a career move for someone whose feet are not tied to a paper. What she says in one-on-ones is cleaner than what her calendar shows.

Once the manager sees it, the work is not to press harder for Level 3. It is to lean on a different rung. More weight to Level 2: *"Here is what I see you handle easily. Here is where I see you working around something. Am I reading that right?"* Level 2 is safer because it is about the work, not about her. And narrow, specific disavowals where they can help: *"Saying you don't want to lead this project doesn't affect your standing here."*

She may never become expansive. Level 3 may stay out of reach. What is in reach is a more accurate read of the work, and a relationship where she escalates blockers earlier and pushes back on bad plans in writing. That is the version of trust she can afford.

The prescription *"go deeper with each person"* assumes going deeper is available to both sides. Under steep asymmetry it is not. The ethical move, more often than the ambitious one, is to climb only as far as the person can afford to climb with you.

The Curiosity Trap

Not every relationship should go to Level 5. The goal is to know enough, and the right things, to manage each person well.

Some people will invite the climb slowly. Some will never want their manager that close, and that is their call to make. A good manager helps without demanding unnecessary revelation.

Your curiosity is not morally self-justifying. It can feel like care and still be mostly about you. *"I want to understand who you really are"* is a harder request than it sounds, and the person on the other side of it does not get to decline without cost. Not all useful management needs biography. Some of your best reports want precision, fairness, and clean support more than they want a relationship with you. Pushing for more than that, and reading their polite acceptance as consent, takes something they did not agree to give.

A manager gets to ask what a report cannot ask back. *How are you, really? What drives you? What are you afraid of?* These are not neutral, because the person asking them can decide next quarter's assignment, and the person answering them cannot ask the same of the person across the desk. Every climb up the Ladder is structurally one-way. The report can make themselves legible to the manager; the manager does not have to return the favor at the same level. That is not a failure of the relationship. It is its shape. The move the restraint asks for is to hold that shape in mind and not pretend it isn't there.

The Distance Trap

The opposite mistake costs people too. In staffing meetings I have watched the cost of *not* knowing people play out many times. The managers who could speak at length about a report (naming what they were good at, where they were stuck, where they wanted to be in two years) placed that report well. The managers who had only a sentence or two about a report spoke for them in a sentence or two, and when the list got cut down, those were usually the names that moved.

Most of the managers doing this were well-meaning. The difference was fluency. A manager who knew someone at Level 3 or Level 4 could argue for them in detail, could match them to a project, could push back when someone else reached for their name. A manager who only knew someone at Level 1 or 2 had a shorter argument available. The quieter report whose manager could not argue in detail was the easier name to move off a roster. Nobody in the meeting decided the private report was weaker. The argument for them was simply thinner, which produced the same outcome.

They paid for that thinness in assignments they never heard about. A project one of them would have grown in went to the person whose manager had three minutes of vocabulary ready. In a promotion round, the legible report's readiness was said aloud, and the private report's readiness was assumed to be lower because nobody in the room could describe it in the moment. The private reports did not learn that their own manager's thin description had done the arguing against them.

The prescription is not to force access with every report so that your advocacy is even. Some reports want to be known that way and some do not, and the rest of this chapter is about holding that line. The prescription is to notice that access is unevenly distributed on your team, and to make sure the unevenness is not doing your staffing for you. If you have less to say about someone in the room, prepare more before the room. Write a few sentences down. Ask the teammate who works with them what they have seen. Come in with something to say about everyone on your team, so that the silence after a name is not an argument you did not know you were making.

The Collector of Confessions

The cost of *not* knowing your reports is one half of the picture. The cost of misusing what you know is the other.

The most common failure of restraint is the smallest one. Over a year, a report tells you a handful of things. A parent who is sick. A project at their last company that made them wary. A reason they have been underplaying themselves. You hold them, and you remember. In a staffing meeting two years later, you mention, gently, that this person probably should not take the international assignment because the family situation is not stable. You do not cite the disclosure. You do not need to. The sentence carries it. The person is not in the room. They never know.

That is the quiet, almost considerate version of becoming a collector of confessions. And it does the damage quietly too. A manager can accumulate knowledge about someone across years and start to use it, not maliciously, not even consciously, but in ways that narrow the person's options without their consent. Disclosure that was a moment of trust becomes context that shapes decisions the report does not get to see. From the report's side, extraction rarely looks like extraction. It looks like a manager who remembers more than the report thought they did. It looks like a comment in a one-on-one (*"I know you were hoping for that project"*) that references something never said out loud to this person. It looks like the feeling, not quite articulated, that the manager is slightly more possessive this quarter than last. None of it crosses a line the report could point to. All of it adjusts what the report brings next time. The next disclosure, if there is one, is slightly shorter.

Imagine a staffing meeting in October. Six people around a table with a spreadsheet open. The row that has everyone's attention is a six-month assignment in Dublin. High visibility, the kind of thing that accelerates a career. Three names are under consideration. One of them is your report, Anita.

Two years earlier, over coffee after a difficult week, Anita had told you her mother was sick. She mentioned it as context for why she had been quieter for a few weeks, not as an ask. She did not bring it up again. It was not a secret; her team knew her mother was not well. But she did not repeat it, and you held the conversation quietly, out of any room she was not in.

Now the room is looking at you. Someone has just made the case for Anita: the Dublin work plays to her strengths, and she is overdue for a stretch assignment. You say, carefully, *"I'd be cautious about Anita on that one. She's got things at home that would make a long stint in Dublin heavy."* The sentence is general. It could mean anything: childcare, a partner's job, a house move. The room takes it in. Two of the others nod. The conversation turns to the second name, and by the end of the meeting Anita's row is unhighlighted.

You believe you have been careful. You did not name her mother. You did not give a diagnosis. You used language vague enough to cover a dozen situations. And the decision is made, on information she gave you in confidence, and she will never hear how it was used.

A quarter later Anita notices she was not considered. She asks you about it. You tell her, truthfully, that it was a close call and the timing did not work out. Both sentences are accurate. Neither is the whole story.

The sentence you said in the meeting is the visible part of the trade. What matters is the category of sentences that became available to you once she had trusted you with her mother. A manager who reuses confidences this way is not cruel. They have accumulated context over years and started to spend it without deciding to. Each trade is small: one sentence in one meeting, general enough to deny, specific enough to close the door. Across a career, those sentences pile up into assignments the report was never in the room for.

The other common reuse happens inside the performance conversation itself. Imagine a report named Jordan tells you, in a one-on-one in March, that he was running on fumes through most of the previous quarter. Something at home had been eating more than he was used to giving. He is not asking for anything, just explaining why his output had felt less than it could have been and why he had been short in a few meetings he regretted. You take it in. You do not press. Over the next two months you move a deadline, you pair him with someone on the harder part of the project, and by June his energy is back.

By December you are writing his year-end review. The year had a rough middle, and you are trying to explain, in writing, why the trajectory was uneven. The sentence comes easily: *"The first half fell below the bar we had set together, reflecting a difficult stretch, with strong recovery in the second half."* It is a kind sentence. You read it back. You feel good about it.

It is also carrying the March conversation. You did not name the burnout. You did not name the personal thing. You did not have to. The phrase *"a difficult stretch"* is doing the work, and if Jordan reads the review and hears the March one-on-one in it, he will be right to hear it. A shorter writeup (*"the first half was below bar; the second half recovered strongly"*) is a record of what you saw. The longer version is a record of what he said plus a softening gloss.

Nothing in the review was harsh, and nothing in it was untrue. The next time Jordan is running on fumes, he will run longer before he says anything.

The Evidence Line

The line worth holding is narrow. Information someone gave you in confidence is not available to you as evidence. Things you would have seen without them telling you are.

Sort your notes in that order before the next review cycle. Two columns. On one side, what I saw. Missed commitments, the pattern of escalations, the quality of the last three docs, who they paired well with, what they did in the meeting where the project slipped. On the other, what they told me. A hard thing at home, a reason they were wary of one kind of work, a disclosure about a previous manager, a fear they named once. The first column is performance evidence. The second is context that helps you manage them better. The two should not trade places between March and December.

The edge case is the one where a disclosure explains an observed pattern. Consider a report whose output dropped in Q2. In a one-on-one, they told you their partner had been through a medical scare, and they had been sleeping three hours a night for most of six weeks. Now it is review time, and you are asked to explain Q2. The observation is fair game: output was below bar for six weeks. The explanation is theirs. You can note the observation in the review. You cannot use the explanation to soften the rating without their signal, and you cannot use it silently, as unnamed context, to harden it either. If the explanation seems material to the read of the year, ask them directly: *"I want to include the context of Q2 in how I'm framing the year. Are you comfortable with that, and how would you like it described?"* The difference is whether they knew. The disclosure was theirs to keep or to deploy.

When the observed pattern and the disclosure match closely enough that the review seems to cite the disclosure even when you do not, write less. Describe what you saw. Leave the why with the person who told you, unless they signal that they want it included.

When They Don't Want to Be Known

A few signals suggest it is time to hold. The person answers the Level 3 or Level 4 question in brand language (impact, growth, ownership), and the brand language does not change from month to month. They respond well to operational conversations and briefly stiffen when the conversation drifts personal. They came from a prior manager who did not hold confidences well, and you have not yet been there long enough to unwrite that experience. Or you notice the climbing is mostly pulling from your side. It is your curiosity more than their disclosure. In any of these cases, the work is to stop and do the rungs you have differently.

For a person who does not want Level 5, Level 2 done unusually well is often what they were asking for. It takes more specific work than the phrase suggests. It means reading strengths accurately, not warmly. The difference between "*you are great at this*" and "*the way you structure a write-up before you open a doc is the thing this team most relies on.*" It means framing gaps without flattening them. Not "*you struggle with executive communication*" but "*the thing I want you to practice is arriving at a point faster in meetings where the most senior person gives you three minutes.*" It means matching work to what the person can carry this quarter, which means knowing their load outside the project and not asking them to tell you about it in therapy language.

Done this way, Level 2 is not shallow. It is specific, fair, and more useful to the person receiving it than many Level 5 relationships manage to be. The care you would have brought to a Level 5 relationship can be routed through the rungs they have invited, and most of what they need from a manager is there. What they do not need is the version of the Ladder that treats their willingness to be known as a test they can fail.

A senior engineer joined our team a few years ago. He was reliable, careful, steady. He was not cold, but he was not expansive. Our one-on-ones ran exactly as long as they needed to. He came with an agenda, worked through it, and did not volunteer much about his life outside work. When I asked, he answered briefly and politely and we went back to the work.

Earlier in my career, I would have treated that reserve as something to fix. I would have asked more personal questions and lingered longer on the openers. By then I knew better. I stopped trying to deepen the relationship directly and started trying to make the work safer. I clarified expectations more cleanly. I gave feedback earlier and with less buildup. When he disagreed with me in a meeting, I thanked him and changed the plan, and I did not perform the gratitude.

Over the next year, his updates got more candid. He raised issues earlier. He asked for help sooner. He became more willing to say, plainly, when he thought I was wrong. He never became revealing. He did not talk about his fears or his life or the private logic of his ambition.

He trusted me.

He brought me the real state of things sooner. He let me shape his thinking without polishing every edge first. He did not offer intimacy. He offered honesty, which is the form trust sometimes takes when power is in the room.

That was enough. It let me be useful to him. It let him do better work. It let the relationship work without requiring it to become something it was not.

Two Tests

Two questions test whether the restraint is real. Who does the next rung serve? Them, or the part of you that would feel better if they revealed more? And if they declined the next step, would they pay for it in how you manage them next month? If the answer to either is not clean, the Ladder has started working for you instead of for them.

> *Sometimes the most respectful use of the Ladder is to stop one rung earlier than curiosity wants to go.*

The harder half of the practice is knowing what should not be pushed, and building a relationship that works without it.

Three Ideas to Carry

- **What you learned in confidence is not available as evidence.** What you would have seen without their telling is. The line is how you keep access from becoming leverage.

- **The question is not whether you know. It is whether knowing is helping them.** Curiosity is not morally self-justifying. The Ladder works for them, or it works for you.

- **Sometimes the most respectful use of the Ladder is to stop one rung earlier than curiosity wants to go.** Level 2 done unusually well is often what the report was actually asking for.

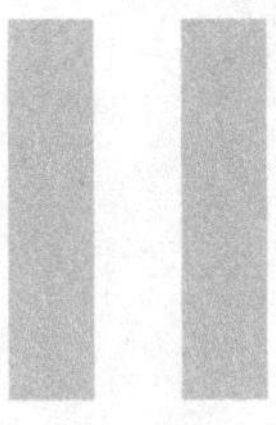

PART II

The Practice of Knowing

The weekly rhythm that takes a manager from task distributor to someone who knows the people they lead. One-on-ones that build trust, the listening that unlocks insight, what drives each person, recognition that fits who they are, and the development that stretches them over the longer arc.

In This Chapter

5

The Weekly Rhythm

"We are what we repeatedly do. Excellence, then, is not an act, but a habit."

— Will Durant, paraphrasing Aristotle

The Truth Ladder is the map. The weekly rhythm is the walk.

"He wanted to catch up on everything."

OST of what a manager comes to know about a person is learned in the quiet stretches: the weeks between off-sites and reviews, when nothing dramatic is on the calendar and you still have to decide what to do with twenty-five minutes. Knowing accumulates. One conversation does not get you there.

Five directions of attention, spread across a month, in rooms you are already in. No new meeting, no tracker. One week someone gets two of the verbs and someone else gets four. That is normal. The pattern worth watching is over several weeks: if the same verb stays empty for the same person, that is the signal.

Held over months, the rhythm moves you up the ladder. A new report reaches Range (what they can do) in a few months. Drive (what moves them) often begins to surface inside the first year. Horizon and Fears take longer, and only if the rhythm holds. Skip the rhythm and you will not move past Role.

The Five

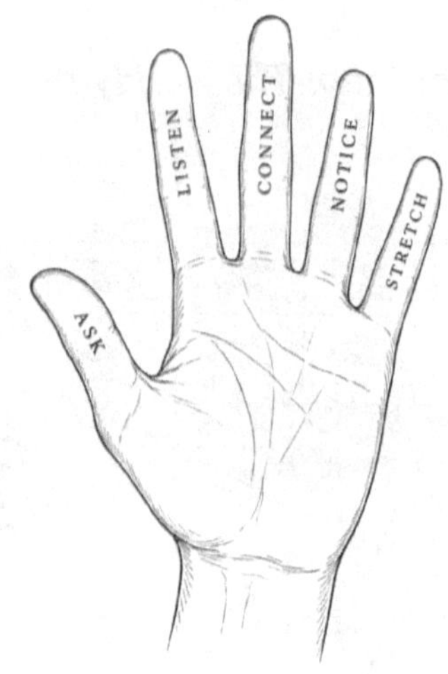

Thumb to pinky: Ask, Listen, Connect, Notice, Stretch.

For each person on your team:

1. **Ask.** What is on their plate? What is in their way? What do they need from you?

2. **Listen.** What is underneath the update? What are they not saying yet?

3. **Connect.** How does the work in front of them tie to something they care about?

4. **Notice.** What did they do well? Name it specifically, while it is still fresh.

5. **Stretch.** What is one thing this week that would grow them?

The Five have a structure. Ask and Listen are receptive: how you draw something out. Connect is the hinge: how you tie the work to what this person cares about. Notice and Stretch are what you give back. Two in, one through, two out.

You won't always do them in order, or in one sitting, and you'll rarely cover all five for every person in a single week. Over a month, the pattern fills out.

Over weeks, different verbs open different truths.

A Week in Practice

Suppose you manage five people.

Anita is a mid-career engineer leading a migration. Steady, private, hard to read.

Jordan is a newer engineer, still learning scope. Eager, fast to ask permission.

Lin is a senior engineer who has said she wants to move into management. She writes the clearest docs on the team.

Rosa is a PM who joined six weeks ago from the commerce team. She is still finding her footing in the domain.

Sam is a designer. Quiet. Does not volunteer much.

Here is one normal week.

Monday. In standup, Lin presents the migration risk breakdown she wrote on Friday. Before moving on, you say, *"The three-class split* *you used there is cleaner than I had in my head. It's going to save us an argument when infra reads it."* Ten seconds. Notice, for Lin.

Later, in Anita's one-on-one, you open with the plain questions. She says the migration is on track and nothing is blocking. You wait. After a pause, she adds that she keeps hitting the same deprecated API and has not wanted to make a thing of it. Ask and Listen, for Anita.

Tuesday. You send Sam a two-line Slack message about the prototype he shared the day before: *"The way you labeled the states in that prototype saved us a round of questions in the review. Thank you."* Notice, for Sam.

In Jordan's one-on-one, he says he is two days behind on a caching task and is not sure he picked the right approach. Ask and Listen. You do not solve it for him. You ask him to walk you through the two options he considered. At the end, you tell him you want him in the spec review for the adjacent auth rewrite. *"You will be a level above where you are comfortable on that one, which is the point."* Stretch, for Jordan.

Wednesday. In a product review, Rosa frames an onboarding issue in commerce language and the rest of the team is slow to catch up. You say, *"The commerce-first frame Rosa is using here is the one to listen to. This team needs more of that kind of reading."* Connect, for Rosa.

In her one-on-one later that day, you ask what would make the role work better for her right now. She says, *"If I had someone walk the funnel with me weekly, I could learn twice as fast."* Ask, Listen, and a second Connect.

Thursday. You ask Lin to run next Tuesday's team sync. Not present at it. Run it. Stretch, for Lin.

Friday. In Sam's biweekly one-on-one, you do the longer Notice: *"What I mentioned Tuesday is not a one-off. You do it every prototype, and the team leans on it even when nobody says so. It's one of your edges."*

Nobody got all five. All the rhythm asks is that you not leave any verb missing for the same person for long.

How It Compounds

A week shows the rhythm in motion. The compounding takes longer.

In Anita's first month, you mostly get Ask and Listen. By month two, you can offer Stretch: you ask her to write up the migration approach for an architecture review board. The document is early and stronger than expected. Notice follows.

By month three, Connect comes through. You tell her you gave her the work because she is the one person on the team who has built a new system while shutting down the old one, and the team needs to see that pattern from someone who has done both. By month four, Listen reaches deeper: a clipped answer in a one-on-one turns, a week later, into the real issue. She had been asked to defend a decision in front of a board that was not hers. By month six, you can ask about Horizon in a career conversation and get a real answer. The approved answer comes first. The real one comes later.

That is what the weekly rhythm does. It turns a person you could describe in role terms into someone whose drive you can name and whose horizon is their own.

Each verb does two things at once: guards against a specific failure, and lowers the cost of a particular truth.

- **Ask** keeps you managing people instead of status reports. It lowers the cost of naming need.
- **Listen** catches the signals that would otherwise be missed. Unfinished thoughts get a place to surface.
- **Connect** keeps the work from drifting free of meaning. It lowers the cost of feeling outside the work.
- **Notice** keeps recognition from being late and generic. Being seen for something real becomes cheap to do.

- **Stretch** keeps years from passing without growth. It lowers the cost of admitting ambition before it is fully formed.

When You Cannot Reach Everyone

You will not practice all five verbs equally with every person every week. The rhythm is not a quota.

The honest question is not *Did I go deep with everyone?* It is *Where would shallow knowledge create the most harm right now?* Some weeks the answer is the new hire who is saying everything is fine. Some weeks it is the high performer who looks worn down. Other weeks it is the quiet person whose work changed but whose updates did not, or the one carrying a visible miss.

When capacity is tight, go deeper where the cost of being wrong is highest. You owe accurate attention, not equal coverage.

The Chapters That Follow

Each verb has a chapter that develops it. **Ask** shows up most often in Chapter 6, the room where the week's questions get asked. **Listen** has its own chapter at Chapter 7. The work of clearing what is in someone's way (where Connect meets Subtraction) is the subject of Chapter 8. The discipline of seeing-and-saying takes shape in Chapter 9. **Stretch** compounds into a career arc in Chapter 10. The pairings are pointers. Each chapter develops its verb but is not limited to it.

Three Ideas to Carry

- The weekly rhythm is a pattern of attention across a month. Treating it as a scoreboard to hit each week misses the point. If the same verb stays missing for the same person three weeks running, the pattern is the signal.

- Notice is the verb most easily lost. The evidence is perishable: say the specific thing within a few days, or it decays into the generic sentence you will say at the review.

- One Stretch per person per week. More may overload. Less stalls. A harder question, a piece of adjacent work a level up, a meeting they run. The size is small on purpose.

In This Chapter

Three Kinds of Conversation

> *"An honorable human relationship... is a process*
> *of refining the truths they can tell each other."*
>
> — Adrienne Rich, 1977

The one-on-one is not a status meeting. It is the conversation where
truth becomes more or less expensive.

"Go on, I'm listening."

THE one-on-one is where you either learn the people on your team or you don't. It is how you climb the Truth Ladder, and where the **Ask** of the weekly rhythm (Chapter 5) becomes a practice: 25 to 50 minutes with one person, where the point is their success, not status.

The one-on-one lowers the cost of unfinished truth. The half-formed worry, the rough version of a thought, the question the report has been pricing for weeks. None of that travels well in standup. The one-on-one is the place where it can surface before it is finished.

Most one-on-ones never get past the surface. They look like one-on-ones and function like status meetings. Blockers, updates, OK-thanks-bye. Both people leave knowing what they already knew. The ritual is kept and the climb is skipped. Managers consistently overrate these meetings.[1]

The Room Is Not Equal

Every one-on-one runs on two clocks. The manager is tracking priorities, blockers, and follow-up. The report is tracking that too, and something else: *What did the last honest thing I said here do for me? What version of this answer is still safe three months from now?*

The gradient is not the topic of the meeting. It is the background the thinking happens against.

That is why cancellation matters more here than it would between peers. A peer cancelling a meeting is a scheduling fact. A manager cancelling is a signal. Most of the time the manager means nothing by it. The report still has to read it.

Three Kinds of Conversation

Every one-on-one contains three conversations. They differ in what they ask the report to risk.

Outcome. The least risky conversation. Priorities, blockers, next steps. Most reports can participate here without revealing much about themselves. Most managers are comfortable here, and most one-on-ones stay here.

Person. The riskier conversation. How are you, really? What do you need from me that you have not asked for? This is where the report names constraint, energy, frustration, confusion, or need, the things that might change how you see them. Level 3 and Level 4 of the ladder begin to open here.

Three questions carry most of the person conversation's weight:

1. *Where do you feel most constrained?*
2. *Where do you feel most stretched?*
3. *What are we building that you actually care about?*

Ask the same person these questions month after month, and they teach you what normal sounds like. Then you start hearing the changes.

Growth. The riskiest conversation. The destination, the gap, the next stretch. Ambition, uncertainty, and future identity enter the room here. A report may tell you the approved version first, because the honest version can affect how you staff, sponsor, or evaluate them. This is Horizon on the Ladder, and the conversation most often deferred to a quarter that then passes.

Each conversation asks for a different posture. Outcome asks for clarity. Person asks for honesty and space. Growth asks you to think about this person months ahead of where they are right now.

Default to outcome and you never get to the rest. You never climb the Ladder. Motivations stay hidden. Recognition stays generic. Career conversations never happen because the one-on-one never made space for them.

The Five-Part Scaffolding

The five sections move from lower-risk truth to higher-risk truth. Accomplishments are easier to name than fears. Blockers come up before ambitions do. Next week is easier to discuss than next year. The order gives the report a way into the room before asking them to go deeper.

- **Accomplishments.** What went well?
- **Blocked items.** Where are you stuck?
- **Next week.** What matters most?
- **Areas to develop.** What are you learning?
- **Quarterly goals.** Where do we stand against the bigger commitments?

Use the structure until you no longer need it. A new one-on-one benefits from the list. A practiced one uses it lightly. Both of you already know the three conversations underneath.

Two Managers, Two One-on-Ones

Sam shipped a platform migration last Friday after six hard weeks. This week's one-on-one is the first one after launch.

Manager 1

The conversation between Manager 1 and Sam.

Manager: Hey Sam, how's it going?

Sam: Good. You?

Manager: Same. Congrats on shipping last week.

Sam: Thanks.

Manager: Any blockers this week?

Sam: Not really. I'm cleaning up the post-launch tickets.

Manager: Good. What matters next week?

Sam: Monitoring dashboards, I think.

Manager: Yep. Anything else I should know?

Sam: No, I think I'm good.

Manager: Great. Good job last week.

Sam: Thanks.

Manager 2

Now consider the same conversation run by a different manager, with the same Sam, the same week.

Manager: Hey Sam, how's it going?

Sam: Good. You?

Manager: Honestly? A little flat. Launches always leave me there for a few days. You?

Sam: (pause) Yeah. A little the same. I thought I'd feel more done.

Manager: Say more.

Sam: I don't know. Six weeks of pushing, and then Monday felt like any other Monday. And Alex not being here makes the cleanup weird.

Manager: How are you doing with that — not the tickets, the Alex part?

Sam: It's fine. He had to do what was right for him. It's just... we'd been working together on this for a year and a half.

Manager: Yeah. That takes longer than you think.

Sam: (pause) Can I ask you something?

Manager: Yeah.

Sam: I've been thinking about whether I want the monitoring work next, or whether I should try to move toward something else. I don't know yet. But I wanted you to know I'm thinking about it.

Manager: Thank you for saying that. Let's use some of next week's time to walk through it. You don't need to have an answer yet.

Sam: Yeah. That works.

What the First Manager Missed

Nothing in the first one-on-one is technically wrong. The manager showed up, congratulated the work, checked blockers, confirmed next week's priorities, and ended on time. This is the one-on-one most managers run most weeks.

What went past: a flattened tone, a careful answer, the absence of anything real. The manager heard the update and missed the gist.

What the Second Manager Did

The second manager did three things.

Went second. *"Honestly? A little flat"* made room for a less polished answer.

Followed the signal. Sam mentioned Alex and the manager did not move on. He went toward it.

Left the future open. When the career question surfaced, the manager did not force clarity. He held the door open for next week.

That is what a one-on-one is for. The point is to make the next truthful sentence cheaper than the safe one.

The Employee Owns It

The one-on-one belongs to the employee. If the manager owns the agenda, talks most of the time, and closes each issue with advice, the meeting becomes a disguised status review.

Ownership matters because the room already belongs to the manager structurally. It is on your calendar, inside your reporting relationship, with your evaluation power sitting quietly in the chair. Letting the report shape the agenda does not make the room equal, but it gives them a piece of agency inside a room that is not equal.

> *The person with less power needs more room to think out loud.*

A useful default is 20/80: the manager talks about 20 percent of the time and the employee talks about 80 percent. Silence is the cheapest way to hand back the room.

Going First Opens the Person Conversation

Structure and sharp questions take you to Level 2 of the Ladder. The higher rungs open only when the manager goes first.[2]

I once had a team member whose behavior had become unpredictable. Late arrivals, flashes of frustration in meetings, arguments out of proportion to the moment. I gave feedback on each symptom as it surfaced. Nothing changed. During one one-on-one, I finally said I had been wanting to bring something up for a while but had not known how. I told them I might get it wrong, then asked if we could talk about the thing underneath. We did. We did not fix it in one sitting, but the relationship shifted that day. My willingness to say *I don't know how to do this, but I want to try* gave them permission to be honest in return.

The manager who never shows vulnerability turns the one-on-one into an evaluation. The manager who goes first turns it into a conversation.[3]

Better Questions for Outcome and Growth

Three habits do most of the work here.

Ask **what** more often than **why**. *Why did that slip?* sounds like a search for a culprit. *What got in the way?* opens the conversation.

Respect the **second answer** more than the first. The first is often the safe version. The second is often closer to the thing.

Resist the **fix-it reflex**. When someone describes a problem, you'll feel the pull toward *Here's what I'd do* early. Ask one more question first.

The full discipline lives in Chapter 7.

Making It Real

Weekly is the right cadence. Less frequent than that and the shared context thins out; you lose track of what mattered two weeks ago. The meeting does not need to be long: twenty to thirty minutes a week gets the highest engagement benefit, at every level.[4] Employees who do not get routine check-ins are rarely engaged at work.[5]

Plan the last two minutes. People judge an experience by its ending more than its average. The employee can leave challenged, even uncomfortable, but should not leave diminished.

One warning: depth beats completion. A one-on-one where you covered all five sections but learned nothing new is wasted. A one-on-one where you abandoned the structure because something real surfaced is the meeting that worked.

When the Outcome Has to Sharpen

Most one-on-ones are coaching conversations. Sometimes they have to sharpen into performance conversations. When that happens, signal the shift early.

"I want to use today's time differently. There's a pattern I'm seeing that I need to be direct about."

Then be specific. Name what you have observed, not what you have concluded about the person's character.

"Over the past four weeks, three deliverables have missed their deadlines and two required significant rework" is an observation.

"You don't seem committed" is an interpretation, and a bad one.

Ask what is happening on their side. Then leave with specific, time-bound expectations and a clear point for the next check-in. The one-on-one is still the right room; only the directness changes.

The Test

A one-on-one succeeds when something true becomes sayable in it that would not have been said anywhere else that week.

Three Ideas to Carry

- **Three kinds of conversation: outcome, person, growth.** Every one-on-one contains all three. Most live entirely in outcome. After every meeting, ask which one you skipped.

- **The meeting belongs to the employee.** Aim for roughly 20 percent talking and 80 percent listening. When you own all the air, you get a status meeting.

- **Go first.** Structure and good questions will take you to Level 2 of the Truth Ladder. The higher rungs open only when the manager shows up honest first.

In This Chapter

Listen for What Wasn't Said

7

"Attention is the rarest and purest form of generosity."

— Simone Weil

Many managers think they're good listeners. Most aren't.

"He considered himself an excellent listener."

THINK of the last time someone listened to you so closely that you came away with a sharper version of your own thinking than you walked in with. They probably did not say much. They might have asked one question. They left space when you paused. You did not feel managed. You felt understood.

Most managers think they do that. Most don't.

This kind of listening lowers the cost of rough thought. The half-formed idea. The worry the report has not yet phrased to themselves. The part of a problem they were planning to skip because it felt too vague to bring.

Years ago we were debating two technical approaches to the same problem. Both were viable. I knew that even as I was arguing. It was one of those design discussions where the technical content was real but the temperature was higher than the stakes deserved. We both had egos to feed.

I pressed hard. I pushed back on every objection. You've probably sat through one of these. Claim, counter, claim, counter, until one side runs out. Then the gotcha. I came back to my points with more conviction each round, and by the end of the meeting I had more supporters in the room. We went with my approach. I thought I'd run a good argument.

Now I can see it was more about winning the argument than about being right. Even that wouldn't have been the worst of it.

Weeks later, writing the implementation docs, I came across a folder of Daniel's notes and design sketches from before the meeting. I had never seen these sequence diagrams. Edge cases I hadn't thought to raise. A scratch document where he had worked through two earlier versions before settling on the one he brought to the meeting. He hadn't been improvising. He'd been thinking this through for a long while. I happened to be the more convincing voice in the room, and I had responded as if he were floating an idea, not presenting one.

I didn't feel the weight of it even then. It had been more than a month. I told myself it was water under the bridge.

I didn't connect what came next to that meeting until much later. During the implementation, Daniel did the work, but he wasn't himself. He was quieter. He wasn't excited about the project. On our daily standups he gave updates like a news anchor, so emotionless I couldn't read him. We were younger then, and I didn't have the experience to know what I was seeing.

Daniel switched teams a few months later. I think he couldn't bear me.

I won't claim the meeting caused it. People leave for many reasons. But I know now what I missed, and the order I missed it in. I missed the weeks of work behind his argument because I was busy winning the argument. Then I missed the disengagement that followed, because I had already decided the issue was settled. I heard everything he said. I didn't understand any of it. He had read the room faster than I had. He saw that I had already won, and that staying in the argument would cost him without changing it.

The skill I lacked that day is the discipline beneath every management conversation. The previous chapter gave you the room. Listening is what keeps it from becoming a status meeting in disguise. In the weekly rhythm (Chapter 5), this is **Listen**, the second verb.

Nobody tells you their deepest professional fear because you ask; they tell you because you have listened well enough, long enough, that saying it out loud feels safe.

The failures are usually subtle. The manager mistakes not interrupting for listening. The diagnostic engine fires at the first plausible explanation, before the person has finished locating what they actually think. A worse version passes for listening. The nod, the *"so what I'm hearing is..."* paraphrase on cue, with no chance the manager's view could change. Ask a room of managers how well they listen and almost every hand goes up.[1] The people who listen worst are the least equipped to notice.[2]

Mirror, Not Wall

The popular image of a good listener is a wall: patient, still, absorbing what you say. The people who listen best do the opposite. You bounce an idea off them and it comes back as a reflection, in the form of questions, sometimes easy, sometimes challenging. You see your own thinking more clearly because someone is holding it up to you.

> *The best listeners are not walls. They are mirrors.*

Wall-listening keeps the room polite. Mirror-listening lets the unfinished thing be said without being penalized for being unfinished.

The questions are exploratory. They help the speaker think, not steer them toward your answer.[3] Being heard clearly changes the speaker on its own.[4]

What this sounds like in a real conversation is small. An engineer tells you he is thinking about leaving the team because he is bored. A wall listens quietly and says *"that's tough, let me know what I can do."* A mirror listens the same way and then asks *"when's the last time you felt the kind of engaged you're missing now?"* And keeps going. *"What was different about that work? Who did you work with? When did the spark go out?"* The questions come back at him until he is looking at his own answer. He may leave the conversation saying *"yeah... I don't know yet."* That is the win. He did not have his own answer when he came in. He has something to think with now.

Listening harder does not mean digging deeper into someone's private life. Honesty is not intimacy. *"What would make this easier to carry?"* is often a better question than *"What is really going on with you?"* The first gives the person room to name what matters. The second can feel like a demand for access they did not agree to grant. Sometimes the ethical move is to stay at the level of the work and let the person decide whether anything else is welcome here.

The Discipline of Silence

Here is a challenge for your next one-on-one: how little can you say?

Not zero. That would be unsettling. But significantly less than you think. Most managers overtalk in conversations meant to focus on the other person. Recorded, they are usually surprised how much of the hour they used.

The gap between the moment someone finishes speaking and the moment you respond is where the real work happens. The person across from you is thinking past their first answer. Rush to fill it and you replace their thinking with yours.[5]

When you ask a question and the person pauses, five seconds, ten seconds, even longer, sit with it. Do not rescue them. Do not rephrase. Do not fill the gap with your own interpretation. The silence is full of the thinking you just prompted.[6]

Two small practices help you hold it. First, the next time you ask a question and get a pause, count silently to ten before speaking. They often fill that silence with something more honest than what they would have said if you had jumped in at second three.

Second, write *why am I talking?* (or W.A.I.T., as it is known) on a post-it above your monitor. Look at it during hard conversations. A post-it outlasts intentions.

Summarize to Their Approval

After silence lets a thought form, summary tests whether you caught it. Paraphrase what someone said in your own words. If they respond "*exactly,*" you have listened. If they correct you, that may be even better. You are in a genuine conversation, both sides working toward a shared understanding.

A report tells you their release keeps slipping. They list reasons: dependencies, flaky tests, a half-written runbook. You listen, then summarize: "*so what I understand is, the real problem is finding time on the operations team's calendar to test.*" They go quiet. "*Yes, that's it.*" A minute earlier they would have named the runbook as the bottleneck.

Listen to summarize the problem, not to solve it.[7] Listening to solve filters every word through your own expertise. Listening to summarize keeps you in their words long enough to hear what they meant.

Don't Try to Fix Them

This is the hardest discipline for any manager. You built your career on solving problems. Someone brings you a problem, and every instinct screams. Solve it. Give the answer. Show your value.

The supplied answer rarely sticks. They follow your steps, maybe, but they have not developed the thinking that would handle the next problem without you. Ask first. *What's actually causing this? What do you know about the other side? What would need to be true for them to prioritize this?* The questions hand the problem back to the person who has to live with it. People remember their own ideas. They forget yours.

Some people push back on the questions themselves. *"Can you just tell me what to do?"* It looks like stubbornness; more often it is time pressure, decision fatigue, or a past manager who used Socratic questions to dodge accountability. Name it. *"I'll give you a direct answer in a minute, but first, one question."* Ask it. Give the answer if it is warranted. The goal is to leave someone thinking more clearly than when they walked in. Sometimes that takes a question. Sometimes it takes a quick answer so the thinking can happen somewhere else.

Articulacy Is Not Truth

Polished language gets read as evidence of clear thought. Chapter 2 names the reason: fluency is partly what people perform when they're talking up a gradient. The less polished account (half-formed, contradictory in places, the one you have to work to follow) often sits closer to what is real.

The signals that matter most get quieter the further up the Ladder you go. At horizon (Level 4 on the Truth Ladder), signals are softened before they leave the mouth. *"I'd be happy staying where I am for now,"* said by someone who a minute earlier described a side project with the only real energy in the one-on-one, is the sound of a horizon put away because it did not feel sayable. At Level 5, fears, they rarely show up in words at all: the engineer who has skipped the last two promotion windows with a different reason each time, the person whose tone shifts whenever a specific kind of problem is mentioned. The more important the thing, the less direct the first telling. The job is to notice which conversations go smaller and widen the room around them.

Receive the polish. Do not reward it. Do not match it by replying with equally composed language. Ask one narrower question a few sentences later, from a different angle. *What would the answer have been if the review cycle weren't next month? What's the version you haven't said out loud yet?* Asked across weeks, they change what the person believes is sayable here. And read the pattern across people. When three reports describe a project in the same careful way (*a growth experience, challenging but rewarding, a lot to learn from*), the phrasing has stopped being about the project. The individual polished answer is not worth arguing with; the pattern is.

The Body Follows Attention

Everything in this chapter can be undone by your body language.

I once had a manager who was a great conversationalist in person. Engaging, curious, warm over lunch. But our one-on-ones were on video, and in front of a computer he became someone else. I could see his eyes scanning text. I could hear him typing. I'd share something I was excited about, and he would nod and say *"yes, mmm, yes, oh really."* Then he would ask a question I had already answered five minutes earlier, the one he had responded to with *"oh really."* I was childishly hopeful each call would be different. It never was.

If you are truly listening, you do not have to think much about posture. The body follows attention, yours and theirs.

When you are not in the same room, the signals are different, but they are still signals. A reply that used to come back in a minute now takes three hours. A Slack thread that used to carry half-formed sentences switches to careful paragraphs. The rough-draft thinking disappears from chat. In person, body language goes flat; in text, it goes formal. The loss of looseness is the signal either way.

Listening When Someone Is Defensive or Angry

A peer once pushed back at me: *"I don't get it. It's urgent. We had to deliver whatever we have."* The deliverable wasn't ready for production. The urgency had been passed down to him without a real explanation, which was why I wasn't convinced. What I should have heard was that he was carrying a deadline he didn't understand either, and we belonged on the same side of the table.

Everything in this chapter gets harder when the person across from you is upset.

They push back on feedback. They shut down mid-conversation. Their voice rises, or goes flat, or disappears entirely. They cross their arms and stop making eye contact. They say "fine" in a way that means the opposite.

Your instinct will be to manage the emotion. Calm them down, correct the record, explain why they shouldn't feel what they're feeling. Every one of those responses makes it worse. Telling someone they shouldn't be upset is arguing with reality, and it signals that their emotional response is the problem. You have made expressing emotion unsafe.

Instead, listen harder. Not to fix. To understand what is underneath the reaction.

Name what you see without judging it. "You pulled back when I mentioned the reorg. What's going on for you there?" Then wait. The silence after that sentence is the most important one in the conversation. If you fill it, you will lose what's underneath it. If you hold it, they will often tell you something they hadn't planned to say, something closer to the actual issue.

Defensiveness usually means someone feels threatened: their competence, their standing, their sense of fairness. Anger usually means something they care about has been violated. The surface emotion is a signal, not the message. Respond to the signal ("calm down," "let's keep this professional") and you never reach the message.

Do not match their energy. If they escalate, stay steady. Your calm signals that the conversation is safe to have. Raise your voice to match theirs and it becomes a confrontation. Stay level and it remains a dialogue: uncomfortable, but productive.

Sometimes the person needs to vent before they can think. Let them. You don't have to agree; you have to demonstrate that you heard it. When the intensity drops, summarize: "It sounds like the main issue is that the decision was made without consulting you, and that felt dismissive." If you get it right, you'll see the tension leave their shoulders. If you get it wrong, they'll correct you, and the correction brings you closer.

This is where listening earns its independence from coaching. Coaching assumes a person ready to think. When someone is defensive or angry, you cannot coach. The nervous system is in protection mode. You have to listen them back to a place where they can hear you.

Three Ideas to Carry

- **The best listeners are not walls. They are mirrors.** A good listener holds your thinking up to you as questions you can think with. Paraphrase what the person said in your own words; when they respond "*exactly,*" you have listened. Your job is to help them see their own answer, not to hand them yours.

- **Listen first, then coach.** Coaching assumes someone ready to think. Listening creates that readiness. Sit with the silence. Ask what they think is happening. People remember their own ideas; they forget yours.

- **Articulacy is not truth.** The fluent report may be rehearsed; the halting one may be closer to the thing. Watch the surface (the flush, the flat voice, the careful phrasing) and read it as signal, not as style.

In This Chapter

8

Motivation Is Subtraction

"The surest way to get someone to do a
good job is to give them a good job to do."

— Frederick Herzberg

Find what is in their way, and clear it.

"The motivation machine was fully stocked."

MOTIVATION is subtraction. What looks like low motivation is usually drive bending around something it cannot push through. A manager's blame, a tool the person cannot access, a customer they have never seen. Most management advice tells you to add things like pep talks, engagement programs, and recognition platforms. That is usually the wrong diagnosis. Instead, you have to find what is already draining the team, and clear it.

The best teams I have worked with did not have more motivated people than other teams. They had fewer blockers between the person and the work.

Fair compensation matters. Pay is a floor. Under it, motivation is not the real conversation. Above it, raises lose their pull faster than most managers expect. This chapter is about what lives above it.

This work lives at Drive, Level 3 of the Truth Ladder. What moves each person, what drains them. You cannot remove a blockage you cannot see, and you will not see what is in someone's way until you know them there. In the language of the weekly rhythm (Chapter 5), this is how **Ask** and **Connect** get applied at Level 3.

This practice lowers the price of admitting something is in the way, including the possibility that you are. People do not volunteer that observation cheaply, and they do not volunteer it at all when the price looks high. Subtraction starts with making the blockage sayable.

You already met the three questions in the Quick Start and Chapter 6. *Where do you feel most constrained? Where do you feel most stretched? What are we building that you actually care about?* Here they're the instrument. Each points at one kind of blockage. A constraint you can remove, a stretch you can hand them, a recipient you can put back in view.

Clear the Constraint

Where do you feel most constrained?

Start here because the constraint is usually the answer. When someone's drive looks low, the most common reason is that something about the work is blocking them from doing it the way they know how. The blockage can be structural, like an approval that takes days or a tool they cannot access. More often it is human. A manager who punishes the wrong things. A colleague who agrees in the room and shoots ideas down afterward.

I watched a team of capable people pull back under a blockage like this.

Marc led five solution architects. He was approachable, easy to talk to when you ran into him in the hallway or the kitchen. From the outside, nothing looked wrong.

One of his architects proposed a design for a deliverable and committed to a timeline. During implementation, the team discovered a missing integration point that created a dependency on another group. That group was stretched thin. The delivery slipped. The internal customer was upset. Marc's response was to announce that no one on his team would give timelines without his review and approval. In the meeting with the internal customer, he spoke after his architect and placed the blame squarely on him. I was in the room. Marc never asked how the estimate had been built. If he had, he would have learned that the architect had consulted the subject matter expert for the system and based his timeline on the documentation he was given. The integration point that caused the delay had been added after the original design and was never properly documented. The architect had done his due diligence. The gap was in the system, not in his judgment. Marc never looked into it. He saw a missed deadline and assigned fault.

This was one incident, but the pattern repeated. Every time a decision led to a problem, Marc blamed the person who made it. The architects learned fast. They stopped proposing anything without checking with him first. Questions that any senior architect should answer on their own got routed upward. Nobody wanted to be accountable for anything, because accountability had become a trap. Everything slowed down. Marc became the bottleneck for every decision, and his team waited for him rather than risk being wrong.

Eventually Marc moved on and a new manager took over. Within a few months, the same architects were making decisions and owning timelines again, moving faster than they had in over a year. The talent had been there the whole time. Marc had been holding it down.

If I had asked any of those architects the constraint question while Marc was still there, the answer would have come immediately. *I cannot make a decision without running it past Marc first, and Marc will blame me if it turns out badly, so I do not make decisions anymore.* The question often works because the blockage is usually visible to the person living with it, even when it is invisible to the manager above them. Ask. They will tell you, when the price of telling is low enough.

Restore the Stretch

Where do you feel most stretched?

Ask this when the work has stopped pulling effort out of the person. Comfort-zone work doesn't pull effort. The ticket gets closed, the engineer goes back to Slack, nothing inside them moved. Work that punishes more than it teaches doesn't pull effort either. Energy lives in the band between, where the work is hard enough to require attention and shaped well enough that the attention pays.

There's an old line: if someone has been doing the same thing the same way for two years, they have not had two years of experience. They have had one year of experience, repeated. Teams fall into this gently. Nobody notices until the energy is gone and the tickets are still being closed.

I watched one engineer come back from it.

For weeks, Leo had been executing steadily: picking up tasks at sprint planning, delivering most of them on schedule, giving flat updates in standup. His voice had the cadence of someone reporting the weather. Nothing late, nothing broken, nothing suggesting he cared about any of it beyond keeping pace. Sprint after sprint, the same rhythm. Take the ticket, do the work, move on. *Is everything okay, Leo? Yeah.*

Then we hit an integration problem nobody had planned for. A third-party library we depended on couldn't handle a specific edge case. Our options were to switch libraries, buy a commercial one, or work around the limitation in our own code.

He suggested a fourth. Fix the library ourselves and send the patch back to its maintainers. It was ambitious and risky. The maintainers might refuse the change, and if they did, we would carry the fix on our own from then on.

I told him to try it. I kept researching commercial alternatives as a backup.

He came back before the end of the week with a working proof of concept. In standup that morning, I could hear the difference in his voice. He walked the team through what he had built and what he had learned about the library's internals. His voice had energy I had not heard before. He completed the full implementation in the following sprint and submitted the pull request to the project maintainers. The first round of review came back asking for changes he disagreed with. He wrote a careful reply, rewrote the parts he thought were fair, argued back on the parts he didn't, and waited. It took a few more weeks than he'd hoped. His fix was accepted.

Something shifted right away, and more followed over the next few weeks. Other people on the team picked up his energy. He started volunteering for ambiguous problems instead of waiting for well-defined tickets.

Nothing about his compensation or role had changed. What changed was that he found a problem worth owning, and someone let him own it.

You usually notice the flatness before anyone names it. The flat status-meeting voice, weeks that look indistinguishable from the weeks before. The stretch question comes after. It checks what you already suspect and lets the person name it in their own words.

The bigger move in this story came before any question would have helped. When Leo proposed the fourth option, I said yes. Flatness breaks when someone reaches. Reaching dies when you say no. Watching for the flatness keeps you ready. The day someone reaches, lean toward yes.

Put the Recipient Back in View

What are we building that you actually care about?

This is the hardest question to ask and the hardest to answer. It is asking a person whether their work has a recipient, a specific human whose day the work touches. When the answer is yes, and the person can picture the recipient, the work keeps its substance even on difficult days. When the recipient disappears, the work goes hollow.

The first answer you get is often the approved one. Mission language, the value statement, the phrase a person has learned to say to managers. The real answer comes later, once the relationship can carry the honest version.

I know what that flatness feels like because I have been inside it.

Very early in my career, I was a Unix system administrator. The job was simple to describe and hard to feel anything about. My team ran hosting for a couple hundred companies. When a new customer signed up, I added the account, pointed the domain name at a virtual IP, set up the mail routing, allocated disk space, and worked through a handful of other pieces that had to be in place before the site could go live. Then the next customer arrived, and I did it again.

I had been doing it long enough that nothing about the work surprised me anymore. The keystrokes were automatic. I could have the whole setup done before the ticket finished loading. I was not learning anything. I was adding lines to configuration files and the lines all looked like the lines from yesterday.

Then a senior engineer named Ahmet joined the team. He knew more than I did technically. That part I expected. What surprised me was the rest. He wanted to know who the companies were and who used their websites. Sometimes he would get on the phone with a customer over a specific request. I thought the request did not need a call. He wanted to understand what the customer was trying to do. He would come back from those calls with details none of us had asked about. One customer was a small publisher whose entire business depended on catalog uploads every Tuesday. Another was a regional news site whose traffic could triple in an hour when a big story broke.

I had been working with the same accounts for months and I had never known any of that. I had a directory structure in my head, not a customer.

One afternoon, working on a routine change for one of those accounts, I saw the work a different way for the first time. I had been thinking of the task as configuration for a company name I recognized and nothing more. What I was actually doing was making it possible for a person on the other end, someone I would never meet, to do their own work. The hosting was the conduit. My config lines were quietly carrying the effort of another person trying to get somewhere. When the site was fast, they were faster. When it broke, their day stopped.

Same tickets, same commands. The thing I was doing had changed.

Ahmet did not need the third question. He started learning who the customers were, and the rest of us started seeing them too. Most managers will not have an Ahmet; the question is how you do deliberately what he did by instinct. When someone on your team cannot answer it, the work has drifted into something they can no longer care about. Drift is easier to fix early, before they stop seeing it from the inside.

Reading the Empty Answer

When all three answers are good, the person's energy is already moving toward the work. Stay out of the way.

When one comes back empty, you have a diagnosis. You can see what is draining the energy. You probably put it there yourself, or it's something only you can remove. The response is attention, not a pep talk or a raise. Change what produced the answer.

Asked month after month of the same person, the questions teach you what that person's *normal* looks like. You start noticing shifts in the answers before the person notices them, and noticing early is what lets you act while there's still time.

When the Thin Answer Is the Answer

Sometimes the answer does not come back empty. It comes back thin. You ask where someone feels constrained and they say *nothing, I'm fine.* The voice is flat; the scope on their last few projects has been shrinking. In standup, they sound like they are reading. You can see the constraint, and they are telling you it is not there.

Do not press the question. An abstract denial, pressed, produces another abstract denial. Go to specifics. *Is there anything in your way?* produces *nothing, I'm fine.* Try *The Redis migration got pushed to next quarter. You were close to it, was that your call?* Specifics are harder to redirect than abstractions. You are giving their honesty somewhere to go.

A thin answer is information. The harder case here is that the constraint may be you. Your decisions, your tone, a permission you withheld, a past moment they have not forgotten. Silence is the cheaper path, and you are the only one who can change the price.

If you cannot find the blockage after specifics, assume it is one you put there and work backwards. Ask what they would change about how you manage them. Ask what a great manager would do differently this quarter.

When Competence Hides Drift

The hardest person to read is often not the struggling one. It is the capable one whose work still looks good while the energy behind it has already gone. They keep delivering because they are disciplined. Saying yes is a habit they built when they were still hungry, and the habit is still running. The manager sees performance and misses drift. This is the drift Chapter 1 warned about, now showing up in someone whose performance still looks fine.

With a high performer, the questions need a sharper edge. *Are you still challenged?* invites the approved answer. Better questions:

- *What part of your work still feels alive, and what part has become maintenance?*
- *What problem would you choose if you could no longer choose the familiar one?*
- *What do people keep coming to you for that you no longer want to be known for?*

The signal is rarely a complaint. It is a flatness in the part of their voice that used to carry energy, a willingness to take the assignment they would have argued about a year ago, a project they used to volunteer for that they now wait to be asked. By the time a high performer hands in notice, the answer to the third question has usually been *nothing, really* for several months.

Three Ideas to Carry

- **Motivation is subtraction.** What looks like low motivation is usually drive routed around something. Fear, boredom, or work with no recipient. Find what is already draining the team and clear it, instead of adding pep talks or incentives.

- **Three subtractions, three instruments.** Clear the constraint, restore the stretch, put the recipient back in view. The questions you already met (*most constrained? most stretched? what are we building that you actually care about?*) are how you read which subtraction the person is waiting for. When any answer comes back empty, that is your diagnosis.

- **Watch the flatness, and lean toward yes when someone reaches.** Flatness sounds like the reporting-the-weather voice in standups and weeks that look like the week before. The shift usually happens before any question. The day someone proposes a harder path than the one you planned, say yes. A manager's reflex is to say not-yet, and the flatness is what that reflex costs.

In This Chapter

Proof That You Noticed

— Mary Oliver

Praise says what you liked. Recognition proves what you saw.

"It had been a while."

RECOGNITION is proof that you noticed. What you say in the moment reveals how closely you have been paying attention. Where Chapter 8 asked how to clear what was in someone's way, this chapter asks how to name what they did well. Both live at Level 3 of the Truth Ladder, where the manager has watched closely enough to say something true about the person's work. In the weekly rhythm (Chapter 5), this is **Notice**, the fourth verb.

Specific recognition lowers the cost of being seen accurately. Under the gradient, a manager's praise is never a clean signal; the report is always pricing it as evaluation, even when nothing else is on the table. The work of this chapter is to recognize in a way that pays that tax down rather than up. That means specific enough that the report can tell you read the actual work, not the gist. Specific enough that they don't sit at their desk afterward asking what you really meant.

Done badly, it is just as revealing. Generic praise tells the person you did not look closely. Public praise for someone who prefers private tells them you do not know them. Asking for their judgment and then going your own way without a word tells them the ask was theater. Every misfit recognition exposes the gap between how well you think you know this person and how well you actually do.

I had dinner once with my skip-level manager. He was two layers above me, and I had no expectation that he knew what I was actually working on day to day. The dinner was with people from across the company. After the usual small talk, he turned to me and asked how the project was going. I gave him the high-level answer, the kind you give a VP you assume cannot follow the details and would be bored if you tried. He listened, then said he had heard the team had built such-and-such, that my own contribution to that piece had been interesting, and that he had been wondering why I had not tried a particular alternative.

I was shocked. Not by the question, but by the fact that he knew. He understood the solution well enough to imagine alternatives. He was curious about the parts I had not chosen. None of this had reached me through any formal channel. He had simply been paying attention. That was recognition. He wasn't even trying.

What the Report Also Hears

Picture a manager passing a report's desk and saying *the way you steadied the team through Tuesday's escalation was exactly the call.*

Thirty seconds later the manager is in the next meeting. The report is still at the desk, replaying the sentence. Did the manager mean it the way it sounded. Will they remember saying it tomorrow. A short written note in the same moment registers differently. The report screenshots it, or keeps the email starred. Thirty seconds on the manager's side. A durable object on theirs.

Recognition from a manager is never quite the same as recognition from a peer. A peer says *nice work* and the sentence is complete. A manager says the same sentence and the report also hears: *I am being noticed by the person who can affect what happens next for me.* Both things register in the same second. In a healthy relationship the observation is welcome. In a newer one, or an uncertain one, or any of the steeper ones — probation, a recent miss, a visa that ties them to the company, a manager the report does not yet trust — the observation costs something on its own. The praise still works. It just does not work cleanly.

That is why specificity matters. Generic praise stays inside the observation and nowhere else. The report hears that the manager was watching, had a thought, and is sharing it, and spends the rest of the sentence sorting what the thought might mean for their standing. Specific praise points to the work. It tells the person the manager saw something about what they did, not something about how they show up. The force that makes *great job* feel hollow in a peer relationship makes it slightly menacing in a manager relationship. The person does not say so.

Written recognition carries more under the gradient for the same reason. A spoken compliment fades, and the report is left with whatever meaning they assigned to it in the moment. A short, specific written note, the kind the person can return to on a hard Friday, is proof the manager can be quoted against later. That permanence is what makes it useful. It is evidence the report can use in a conversation they are having with themselves about whether they are doing alright here.

The Stakes

The cost of doing this badly shows up in turnover. Employees who feel well-recognized are 45% less likely to leave within two years.[1] So ask: has this person heard something specific and genuine about their work in the past week?

How Misfit Recognition Reveals the Gap

Recognition is not only a gift you give; it is also a diagnostic. When it misses, the misfit tells you exactly where the Ladder is short on that person. The signs are usually plain. A face that changes mid-sentence, a colleague who is suddenly less available the next morning, a thank-you that comes a beat too quickly with no specifics underneath. Each kind of failure points at a specific level. You've been treating the person as if you know them less well than you actually do, or more. Read these patterns as data about the gap, not as a sign you've failed at this. Four show up most often.

Public praise for someone who prefers private

The most common misfit. You name someone in a team meeting to honor their work, and they shrink. Their face moves. The next time you reach for them, they are less available. The signal is that you either did not know their preference or you knew it and deployed the general gesture of recognition anyway. The Ladder gap is at Level 2, possibly Level 3: the texture of how this person wants to be seen.

Asking for their judgment, then ignoring it

"*I'd like your take on this.*" Hear the answer. Go the direction you would have gone anyway, without explanation. The person learns the ask was performance. The recognition evaporates in retrospect. The gap is at Level 3: you were reaching for the gesture of recognition without paying the cost that makes recognition real.

Favoring the visible

Recognition drifts toward the loudest contributors, the ones whose work passes through your channels, the ones who remind you of yourself. The quiet engineer who reliably delivers clean code, the operations coordinator who prevents problems nobody else sees, the team member who makes everyone around them better. These are invisible to managers who mistake volume for impact. Track your own pattern: over the past month, who have you recognized, and for what? If the same names keep appearing, the gap is that you have been climbing the Ladder with half the team and barely watching the other half.

Favoritism is personal; inequity is systematic. Fewer than one in three employees strongly agree they receive fair and equitable recognition, with meaningful disparities along racial and gender lines.[1] Most of it emerges from who is most visible to the manager and who speaks up most in meetings. The audit is the same: if entire groups never appear in your recognition log, you have a structural problem that good intent will not solve.

Coupling recognition with criticism

"Great presentation, but next time you should..." The moment you append constructive feedback to recognition, you have nullified the recognition. The person walks away thinking about the criticism, not the praise. Recognition and coaching serve different purposes and belong in different conversations. When you recognize someone, recognize them. Full stop. Save the development feedback for a separate moment.

Does Praise Crowd Out Meaning?

One legitimate worry sits under everything in this chapter: does praise crowd out the meaning people find in the work itself?

You notice it when hallway talk shifts from *what did we ship?* to *who got named in the all-hands email?* The high performer who used to volunteer for the unrewarded work — the doc cleanup, the painful migration, the help they didn't have to give — quietly stops. The crowd-out is rarely dramatic. It is a slow shift in what people put effort into, set by what the system notices.

It can happen. Reward someone for work they already find interesting and, over time, the work itself motivates them less. The effect is strongest when the reward is tangible and contingent, like the gift card tied to a scored behavior or the bonus pegged to a metric. It fades, sometimes disappears, when the feedback is just information about what was seen and why it mattered, with no transaction wrapped around it.[2]

Recognition crowds out meaning when it substitutes for the work being genuinely good. When it inflates the trivial. When it behaves like a compensation mechanism, the transactional feel of points and gift cards. A person doing work they care about doesn't need to be told the work matters. They need to be told it was *seen.*

The corrective is your attention. Start naming the unscored work specifically, in the same channels the scored work gets named in. The system rewards what it can measure. You can choose to notice the rest.

Without the seeing, praise becomes noise. The rest of this chapter assumes the distinction.

Ask for Their Judgment

When you ask someone for their perspective, you are telling them what you have noticed about their thinking. The good version is targeted.

You ask the engineer about the read-replica fan-out because you have noticed she's the one who keeps catching the edge cases nobody else sees. The ask itself is recognition: you are drawing on something specific about how this person thinks.[3]

It is the same move as any good recognition. You name what you have noticed. You signal it matters enough to act on. Then you ask, because you need what they know.

But the ask is only half of it. What you do with the answer decides whether the recognition holds. The misfit above, hearing the answer and quietly going your own way, teaches the person the ask was performance. Act on what you hear, or explain why you went a different way. People who believe their manager acts on their input speak up roughly a quarter more often than those who don't.[4]

Why "Great Job" Means Nothing

I know what generic recognition feels like from the receiving end. Early in my career, I worked on a problem that had no known solution: technically demanding, high stakes, months of effort. I pulled the team together, championed a direction, and we delivered. When it was done, my manager said something like "Great job" and moved on. I cannot even recall the exact words. What I remember is that they had not taken the time to understand what we solved or why it was hard. It was reflex, not recognition.

I had seen the same generic praise handed to others and assumed it was the norm. But when it was directed at something I had poured myself into, it felt different. I did not care about the praise. I cared that someone who was supposed to care about me had not invested the effort to understand what I went through.

Generic praise — *"Great job," "Nice work"* — carries no information; worse, it tells the person you didn't look closely.

Specific praise names the thing: *"The way you restructured the onboarding flow cut drop-off by 18 percent in two weeks."* It tells the person what they did and why it mattered. It also says something quieter underneath: *I was paying attention.*

Even specific praise can miss when it centers the manager: *"I loved how you handled that, reminded me of when I..."* The gravity has shifted.

Say It When You See It

Recognition has a half-life. The further it drifts from the moment, the less powerful it becomes. The employee who handled a difficult client call with composure at 2 PM should hear about it by the end of the day, ideally within the hour. Save it for the next one-on-one and the connection between the specific behavior and the acknowledgment has already dissolved. Save it for the quarterly review and it is no longer recognition; it is administration.

Recognition has to be a reflex. When you see something worth acknowledging, stop what you are doing and say it. In person. In the moment. Three sentences. What they did. Why it mattered. What it tells you about their capability. Under thirty seconds.

Written recognition lasts. A short, specific note gives the recipient something they can return to on a rough week. You do not need to write twenty notes a day; you need the ones you write to be recognizable as yours.

Praise Them Upward

Recognition from a senior leader carries weight because it is rare. It works when it fits and when the leader actually knows the work. When it misses, it does the reverse: it widens the distance instead of closing it. The praise becomes evidence the leader has not been watching, and that distance is hard to undo.

The same skip-level manager whose dinner opened this chapter also showed me the opposite. A few weeks later, I watched him fail at the same thing in front of an auditorium. He walked to the front of an all-hands to present an award. He read through the prepared citation. Then, because he wanted to make it personal, he stepped off-script and added a specific detail about what the team had built.

The detail was wrong. Obviously wrong: the slide behind him had the correct version right there in large type. People exchanged looks. The team being recognized sat with frozen smiles. In the space of one sentence, the whole "*I am so proud of this team*" speech evaporated. Everything before it got reread through a single lens: *he does not actually know what they do.* For those of us who had worked with him up close, the moment was easy to absorb; he had enough credit that a slip read as a slip. For the people meeting him for the first time, it was the only data they had.

The practical move is cheap and most managers skip it: when your direct report delivers something outstanding, forward the details to your own manager. The employee gets two signals at once. My manager noticed, and my manager made sure the people above them noticed too.[5] Peer recognition works the same way. A specific, timely message in a team channel — "*Elena, the way you restructured that pipeline saved us two days this sprint, and the team noticed*" — lasts longer than the hallway compliment.[6]

Calibrate to the Person

The three questions from Chapter 6 tell you what each person cares about; this section is about how they want that caring expressed. The dimensions worth testing are public or private, verbal or written, craft or outcome, peer-visible or quiet. Some light up being named in front of the team; others would rather you never mention them in a meeting. A few respond more strongly to new responsibilities than to any spoken praise, an implied recognition that says *you've earned more.* Most people prefer a mix of public and private.[5]

You will not get the calibration right from experience alone. Ask each person what works for them. Most have never been asked, and the question itself is a form of recognition.

Treat their stated preference as a first draft. The real answer is warped by the gradient between you and the person answering, and it shows up in the pattern, not the words. *"Public is fine"* or *"however you want"* is sometimes the truth and sometimes the report who hates standing up in a team meeting not wanting to contradict the manager's instinct; gratitude under power is often compliance dressed for the occasion. Read the face, not the answer. Watch what they light up under and what they shrink from. If you recognized someone publicly and their face moved one way, file that, whatever they said beforehand and whatever they will say the next time you ask.

Recognition Is the Output of Attention

It cannot be faked or delegated to a platform.

Recognition is what you say when someone did the work well. Without the noticing, the words are just a greeting.

Three Ideas to Carry

- **Recognition is proof that you noticed.** *Great job* and *nice work* tell the person the opposite: that you did not look closely enough to say anything more specific. The better you know someone, the more precisely your recognition fits, and the harder it is to fake.

- **Misfit recognition reveals the gap.** Public praise for someone who prefers private tells them you do not know them. Asking for their judgment and ignoring it tells them the ask was theater. Each misfit is diagnostic; read it as data about where the Ladder is still short.

- **Recognition has a half-life.** The further it drifts from the moment, the less it is recognition and the more it is administration. Three sentences, within the hour, beats a polished paragraph saved for the review cycle.

In This Chapter

Give Them the Work That Grows Them

> *"And the day came when the risk to remain tight in a bud was more painful than the risk it took to blossom."*
>
> — Anaïs Nin

The work someone can do is not always the work they want to become.

"He gave it everything except room."

Career development lives at Horizon, Level 4 of the Truth Ladder. You cannot give someone the right work without first knowing where they are trying to go. In the weekly rhythm (Chapter 5), this is **Stretch**, the verb that compounds.

Arda joined the team a few weeks into a project. He had four or five years of experience, but none of it was in automation. We had a gap that needed filling, and I needed another pair of hands fast. I walked him through the work, the scope, and the senior engineer who could help him get started. Then I asked, "Do you think you can take this on?"

He said yes.

He meant it. From the first week, he dug in. He worked closely with the senior engineer, learned fast, and got good. A few months later he barely needed help. Soon he was identifying gaps I had not seen, proposing solutions, disagreeing with a senior engineer on a design decision, and turning out to be right. I started thinking of him as the automation lead, because that was what he was becoming.

Then one Monday he asked for a meeting and told me he wanted to leave the project.

I thought something must have gone wrong. Instead, he said the thing I had never asked well enough to hear: "I don't enjoy automation. I never wanted to do it. What I actually want to do is development."

He had spent nearly a year growing in work he did not want. I had never asked what he wanted; I had asked what he could do. He had said yes because he was new and trying to be useful. I had read competence as desire, and the two were not the same thing.

Don't Confuse Competence with Desire

Someone excelling at work they do not want will eventually leave, and you will not see it coming. The signals you think you are reading — ownership, initiative, visible growth — are signals of conscientiousness, not fit.

You have to ask.

A new hire will often say yes to work they can do because saying anything else feels expensive. That is not deceit; they wouldn't lie about what they can do. They just can't yet say no to work they can.

It is the look of a careful answer from someone whose footing is still new.

The Approved Horizon and the Honest One

Most career conversations fail because the manager runs them as a brainstorming session, forgetting that the report is running them as a risk assessment.

The standard advice is to keep career conversations separate from performance reviews.[1] On paper that distinction matters: one looks forward, one looks back. From the report's side of the desk, the two are never truly separate. The person asking *"Where do you want to be in three years?"* is the same person who decides their bonus, their next project, and their promotion readiness. Confuse the two from your side and the report protects themselves anyway: they tell you the ambition that sounds promotable, not the one that is true.

That gradient is why the first answer to *What do you want?* will almost always be a polished version. Call it the approved horizon, the answer optimized for the person who writes the review. More scope, more leadership, faster impact. It is exactly what a strong employee thinks a good manager wants to hear.

The honest horizon is held back. Wanting to master a craft without managing people. Wanting to coast for a year after a burnout. Wanting to transfer to a different department entirely. It might sound like a good idea to ask better questions so they will reveal the honest one. But actually, your job is to prove, over multiple conversations, that the honest horizon is safe to say out loud.

This practice lowers the cost of admitting ambition before it is fully formed. And admitting the version of it that is not promotable. People walk into career conversations already knowing which answers are safe.

Career development goes bad in another way too: the conversation drifts into being a conversation about promotion. Few practices move retention and engagement more than real development, but only when development means growth, not a title the manager cannot promise.[2] The practice that scales is short, frequent, forward-looking conversations integrated into the normal flow of work; ten minutes inside a regular one-on-one is enough when the conversation is focused.[3]

Don't Ask for the Five-Year Plan

If you ask someone for their five-year plan, you will get a performance. Most people don't know exactly what they want, and if they do, they aren't going to hand their deepest ambitions to a manager they do not yet fully trust. The open prompt — *"What are your goals for the next three to five years?"* — is the question most likely to produce the approved horizon.

Reflect what you have noticed and ask them to steer.

"You've lit up every time you've had to untangle a messy data pipeline this quarter, but you looked tired when I asked you to present the roadmap. Am I reading that right?"

That is how you open a career conversation. You use what you already know about their range and their drive to invite them into the horizon question. You are asking them to validate or correct a pattern that is already showing, not to invent a pristine future for the person who writes the review. Once the energy and the drain are named in their own words, the question of *where to go next* builds itself.

This requires restraint. The instinct, especially for experienced managers, is to advise too early. *You should aim for principal. You'd be great in product. You should manage people.* People stop pushing through hard work the moment the reason for doing it belongs to someone else.

Restraint also limits how far in you go. A career conversation does not give you ownership of someone's whole life. You are responsible for the part of their future the work touches. That is enough. You can ask what kind of work they want more of, what they want to learn, what they want to avoid becoming. You do not need to turn the conversation into a confession. Honesty is not intimacy.

How the Approved Horizon Sounds

Even when you start from a pattern, the report may still translate the answer back into approved language. Listen for phrases that sound strong but may be protective:

- "*I want more scope*" may mean *I think that is what ambitious people are supposed to want.*
- "*I want to lead*" may mean *I do not know another way to be valued here.*
- "*I am flexible*" may mean *I do not yet believe I can say no.*
- "*Whatever the team needs*" may mean *I am still earning permission to have a preference.*
- "*I want to stay technical*" may be deep craft, or may be aversion to people leadership. Do not assume either.

None of these are dishonest. They are first-pass answers in a conversation whose stakes the report is already pricing. Treat them as the opening, not the conclusion. The subtler answers come later: more range and less stress, deeper craft over broader scope, a role that fits a life that has changed. You hear them only if the person has learned, over time, that saying them will not cost them.

That is why the career conversation cannot be a one-off. Ask once and you get the performance. Ask on a rhythm, and let the early answers pass without penalty, and what you hear changes.

> *Promotion is a finite resource tied to market conditions. Development is not.*

Give Them the Right Project

The most useful thing a manager can do for someone's career is give them the right project. A real problem with real stakes that forces them to do work they have not done before. Readiness is built by experiences like running something end to end, working across functions whose incentives do not match yours, facing a customer directly, and making a decision under uncertainty. Training cannot replicate what certain kinds of work teach. What experiences alone cannot do, a sponsor often can. Mentors advise; sponsors act. They put their reputation behind the person to get them introduced, assigned, or seen.[4] Vague encouragement — *"You'll get there"* — is what avoidance sounds like.

Soon after a team call in which I talked about side projects as a way to grow, Leena messaged me. She said she was interested and asked whether I had anything in mind. We had not worked directly together before. The obvious gap for her was leading through ambiguity: defining a problem, choosing a direction, and being accountable for the result.

I had an early-stage side project in mind: a framework for designing internal systems. It was still undefined. The faster path would have been to give it to someone senior. I gave it to Leena instead.

At first, our meetings were mostly me explaining and her listening. Her first deliverable missed the mark. A few weeks later she came back with a long list of questions, some basic, some sharp. I told her to keep asking. If she kept asking at that level, she would know the area better than anyone else on the team.

We met every two weeks. Early on, she would describe a problem and wait for me to define the approach. A few months later, she was walking me through options she had already evaluated and asking me to poke holes. When it came time to present the framework more broadly, she organized the meeting, the slides, the message, and ran the presentation herself.

By the time she asked whether I would support her promotion case, the case was already there. She had grown into work that ran on judgment rather than instruction.

That is what a stretch assignment looks like from the inside.

Stretch Assignments

When senior executives are asked to name the experience that grew them most, the answer is overwhelmingly the stretch assignment, above mentoring, classroom training, and exposure to senior leaders.[5]

A stretch assignment is also a test of your accuracy. Too small, and you confirm what the person already knows about themselves. Too large, and you turn development into exposure. Misaligned, and you grow them toward a future they do not want. The sizing is where range — what the person can actually do today — earns its keep.

The art is in that sizing. Too far beyond the employee's capability produces panic or failure. Too close to current skill produces boredom. The right stretch sits in the zone where the person can succeed, but only with effort, support, and some tolerance for discomfort.[6]

The other half of the work is what you do once the assignment is in flight. A stretch project means the person will make decisions you would not have made and miss things you would have caught. If those mistakes hit their performance review, or if you take the project back at the first sign of trouble, you have taught the team that *growth opportunities* are traps with consequences attached. Stretch assignments require you to absorb the risk when the person stumbles. Use your authority to widen the margin of error, not narrow it. Without that, *stretch* is just a higher bar with the same review attached.

Job rotations take the same principle further. Moving someone into a different role for a defined period often produces higher satisfaction, stronger performance, and lower burnout.[7]

The High Performer Trap

The easiest way to lose a high performer is to keep rewarding them with more of the work they have already outgrown.

Because they are reliable, you give them the critical project. Because they are fast, you give them the rescue. Because they are trusted, you give them the ambiguous mess. Each assignment is rational. Together they can become a cage.

The harder question is *What future does this assignment move them toward?* If the answer is *the same future, with more weight,* you may be cashing their strength without growing it.

This is also where recognition can do hidden damage. *"You are the person I can always count on"* sounds like praise. To someone who has become the team's permanent rescue path, it sounds like a jail sentence. The career conversation is where you check whether the work you have been giving someone is shaping the future they want, or just confirming the role they have started to feel stuck inside.

Help Them Move

Bad managers hoard talent. The best are willing to lose it in order to be worth working for.

Most career advice assumes one direction: up. Real careers move sideways, down, across functions, out and back. Aspirations often include moves the person has not said out loud yet, like a lateral into a different function, a sabbatical, a step back that opens a later door. You hear those before the recruiter does, but only if you have been listening.

Most organizations say internal mobility matters. Most employees say they do not actually have opportunities to move.[8] The barrier is usually the manager.

The Rhythm of the Horizon

Career development is not an event. It is a rhythm, and it needs its own meeting, separate from the weekly one-on-one.

Twice a year, put 45 minutes on the calendar specifically for horizon. Do not mix it with project updates. Do not mix it with performance feedback. The separation tells the employee that their trajectory has its own weight here. The toolkit's *Career Conversation Guide* has the questions for the meeting itself; the discipline is mostly in protecting the meeting and showing up to it without the project clipboard.

In between those sessions, growth stays alive in the margins. It is the five-minute check-in inside a regular one-on-one — *How is the presentation work coming?* — not framed as a status report on a development plan. It is the scanning you do in conversations they are not in: catching a messy, ambiguous project three layers up and thinking, *this is exactly the chaos Maria needs to learn how to lead.* The development happens before the next dedicated conversation; the conversation just names it.

The most common failure is the opposite of neglect. The manager runs one sincere career conversation, then spends the next year handing out identical weekly assignments. Growth gets delegated to a conversation instead of built through the work. I think of this as career theater. Caring about someone's career is not the same as shaping what they do this week.

When Growth Stalls

Not every stall is the same.

A senior engineer once asked me to mentor him because he felt his growth had stalled. I suggested he speak at an upcoming event. He agreed. As we prepared, a pattern kept surfacing. Whenever he talked about work, the problems were always outside his control. A difficult client, a missed deadline, a broken process. The reasons were real. None of them was the reason.

I eventually told him that if he wanted my help, he had to come without excuses. I tried everything in this book: stretch work, questions, direct feedback. None of it was the missing piece, because the missing piece was not something I could give him. He had to face his own role in being stuck. That kind of work no one else can do for you.

Some people need more time. Some are in the wrong role. Some were moving well until something changed. A missed promotion, a broken promise, a toxic colleague, a personal situation consuming the energy the job used to get.

When the pattern is clear, the conversation has to be direct: *"I have noticed that the development goals we set in January haven't moved. I want to understand what changed and whether this role is still where you want to invest your energy."*

Sometimes the answer is that the person needs to leave. Start that conversation before it becomes a termination. The team watches what happens when things get hard.

When They Leave

Some of the people you develop will leave. The pull of an outside offer is often not the pay. It is the role the pay makes available.

Sometimes the most honest career conversation ends with the person leaving. That is not a failure of development. It may be its proof. If you know someone well enough to help them see that the next honest step is not inside your team, the work has done what it was supposed to do.

The undeveloped employee who stays spreads stagnation. The developed employee who leaves tells the market your team is where people grow. That is still a better outcome.

Three Ideas to Carry

- **Don't confuse competence with desire.** Someone excelling at work they do not enjoy will eventually leave, and you will not see it coming. Ask what they want before you read what they can do.

- **The first answer is the approved horizon.** Open prompts under power produce the promotable answer, not the true one. Reflect what you have noticed and ask the report to steer; let the honest horizon emerge across conversations, not in one.

- **Stretch requires absorbing the risk.** A real project is the most valuable thing you can give. It only works if the manager widens the margin of error while the person stumbles, instead of letting the mistakes show up on the review.

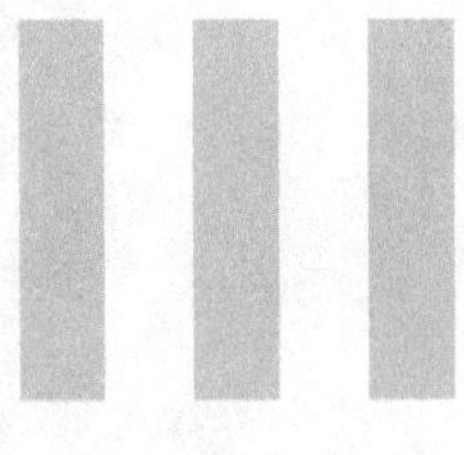

PART III

The Team Around the Work

Knowing your people gives you the foundation. These chapters are about what you shape around them. The clarity of outcome that reaches each person through what you know. The trust between peers that holds the team together when you are not in the room. Keeping the context alive as the work scales. And the relationship with the person above you, where the Truth Ladder runs in both directions.

In This Chapter

Be the Translator

Specify the What, Trust the How

The Four Parts of Context

Context, Control, Abdication

When More Context Is Needed

Translate Through the Person

The Questions I Check Myself On

Make Them Decide

Three Ideas to Carry

The Context Frame

Specify the outcome. Trust the path.

"I also prepared a simplified version."

KNOWING the people is the work the job depends on. It is not what the job produces. Outcomes are the product, and an unclear outcome turns capable people into a team pulling in different directions without knowing it.

This part is about the frame you build around the work: the outcome you specify, and the way you translate it so every person on the team can act on it.

A few years ago, when I was running a hiring push, I learned how easily clarity can be assumed and absent at the same time. We needed to scale the team fast, which meant hiring faster than we had before, especially for some roles. The traditional process was too slow, so we assembled a small tiger team: four people, including myself, who would conduct interviews full-time until we hit our numbers. A dedicated recruiting team sourced candidates and kept the pipeline full. We ran phone screens, then a series of one-on-ones. The funnel was healthy. Candidates were flowing in.

But the pass rate was wrong. Compared to the volume of candidates entering the pipeline, far too few were making it through. I assumed the talent pool was weak. We sat down with the recruiting team to review resumes together, making sure qualified candidates weren't being filtered out before they reached us, and that unqualified candidates weren't slipping through either. We tightened both ends a little, but the real problem was somewhere inside our interviews. So I sat down with one of the other interviewers to understand how his phone screens were going.

His questions were close to mine. He believed certain technical areas were critical, and if a candidate wasn't strong there, they shouldn't advance. I talked to the other two interviewers. Same conviction, different areas. Each of us had a clear picture of what "good" looked like for this role, but the pictures didn't match.

We all knew the job title. We all knew the team needed engineers. What we hadn't defined was what the role required for this team, this seniority, the problems they were solving. The same title carried different expectations across different teams in the same company.

Once the problem was named, we stopped interviewing for a day and built a shared rubric. We wrote down what the role required by team and seniority: which competencies were essential, which were preferred, and which could be developed after hiring. The document wasn't long, but it forced alignment that four experienced people hadn't achieved before.

The pass rate improved. So did the quality of the process. When four interviewers evaluate against the same criteria, their collective judgment is sharper than any individual's instinct.

The problem was clarity, not talent. Assumptions were filling the gap without us realizing. Four people in the same room, working toward the same goal, pulling in four different directions. Context is what keeps a team from solving the wrong problem efficiently.

The gap between thinking you have clarity and actually having it is where most organizations lose their people. The same trap that caught four interviewers in one room catches whole organizations when teams inherit strategy without translating it. Research by Robert Kaplan and David Norton found that only five percent of employees understand their company's strategy.[1]

You know the pattern. The detailed kickoff, the why-slide at the all-hands, the thoughtful email that signals the manager has put in the work. Everyone nods. Three weeks later people are building different things. I call this clarity theater. Clarity is measured by what the other person could now explain to someone who wasn't in the room.

You cannot fix every ambiguity above you. But you can build a bubble of clarity around your team. You can be the translator: you absorb the ambiguity from above and hand the team something they can act on. Your people know the strategy, see how their work connects to it, and can make decisions within that frame. Context is what lets a team decide and act without waiting for you. The team you build that way keeps deciding well after you have moved on.

Be the Translator

Every organization has a strategy: a hierarchy from vision and mission down through goals and action plans. Most of that hierarchy is meaningless if it does not reach the people doing the work, and the primary channel by which it reaches them is you, the manager. Your team is more likely to hear about strategy from you than from anyone else.

Your job is to absorb the ambiguity above (the shifting priorities, the political noise, the directives that changed meaning between the executive offsite and the all-hands) and turn it into a clear, actionable picture for the people below. Not a perfect picture. An actionable one. Take the pieces that exist (the mission, the quarterly goals, the customer outcomes, the things leadership is worried about) and build a version of the direction that makes sense to your team. Repeat it until they can recite it back to you. Then get out of their way.

Take a sentence like *every workload in the new environment by March, no customer-facing downtime*. A senior engineer motivated by deep technical work hears six months of interesting cutover problems. A product lead motivated by customer impact hears a high-risk change that must protect the customer through every step. Same words, different internal arguments. The deeper you know each person, the more precisely you can frame the same strategy in terms they already care about.

Specify the What, Trust the How

The most useful thing I ever handed a delivery team was one sentence long. Not the strategy itself, but the objective the strategy was meant to hit. That was the point.

Years into my consulting career, I was running a large migration for a customer. We had produced a thoughtful twenty-page strategy document, the kind that proves how much analysis went into the plan.

Nobody on the delivery team read past page three. Being thoughtful was the norm; being read was not.

We replaced it with one sentence: *"Every workload runs in the new environment by March, with no customer-facing downtime."*

That sentence showed up on dashboards, in standups, and in every trade-off discussion for the next six months. When an engineer asked whether to delay a migration to refactor a legacy service, the team didn't escalate. They checked the sentence. Would the refactor cause customer-facing downtime? No. Would it push past March? Yes. Decision made.

Most trade-offs are not this clean. A sharp sentence does not answer every question, but it forces every question to relate to the same thing.

The sentence worked because it did two things. It specified the outcome the customer needed. And it trusted the team to figure out the path.

The principle sounds easy and is hard to practice: specify what needs to happen, then trust the team to find the way. Most managers reverse it. They specify the how: the method, the sequence, the tool, the format, the font size on the slide. The what stays implicit. Then they wonder why nobody on their team takes initiative. Initiative requires knowing what you are aiming at and having permission to choose the route.

The distinction worth holding is the one between intent and orders.[2] Orders say what to do. Intent says what the orders are for. A team that understands the intent can adapt when the orders stop making sense in the field. A team that only has orders keeps executing them even after the situation has changed.

> *If you get five different answers from five people, you have a clarity problem, not a motivation problem.*

You can test whether you are specifying the outcome clearly enough by asking any person on your team what success looks like. Fix the sentence before you fix anything else. Clarity does not mean writing more. It means writing less, more carefully.

The Four Parts of Context

Good context has four parts arranged around the work. Two locate it: the why behind, the win ahead. Two define it: the boundaries around, the how within. These four are the frame a team can act inside without you in the room. Miss any one and the work goes sideways in a specific, predictable way.

The why. Why this matters now. What changed in the business, on the team, in the environment that made this the priority this quarter instead of another. The why is what keeps execution from feeling arbitrary. People will carry weight for reasons they understand.

The win. What success looks like, in words a team member could repeat to someone who wasn't in the room. Not a target with seven dimensions; one sentence they can remember. The win is what every trade-off gets measured against when you are not there to decide.

The boundaries. What cannot be violated: a quality bar, a hard regulatory deadline, a dependency the team has to honor, the downstream group that inherits the code on Monday. Boundaries are the part managers most often leave implicit, usually because they assume the team already knows.

The how. The part of the decision space that belongs to the team. Method, sequencing, tool, the internal trade-offs inside the guardrails. The how is what separates context from control. It is the space where the team's judgment lives.

Missing the why: people execute without commitment. Missing the win: they produce the wrong thing, confidently. Missing the boundaries: they hit a wall late, having made a dozen correct decisions that led them to the wrong destination. Missing the how: they produce exactly what you asked for instead of what you needed.

Most managers leave one of the four implicit without realizing it. The boundaries are the most common. People assume the constraints are obvious because they are obvious to them; they forget the team does not see what the manager sees.

Context, Control, Abdication

Context is the middle position in a three-way choice.

Control sounds like "*Here is exactly how to do it.*" You pre-decide every question. The team executes a plan you built. They bring you no judgment because you asked for none.

Abdication sounds like "*Figure it out.*" You hand over the work without the why, the win, or the boundaries. The team runs in whatever direction the strongest opinion in the project points.

Context sounds like "*Here is what matters, what success looks like, what constraints are real. Now use your judgment.*" You leave room for the decisions that should be theirs, and you give them what they need to make those decisions well.

Every manager has a home drift. Some drift toward control when the stakes feel high. Others drift toward abdication when the work feels uninteresting, or when the team is strong enough that handing off with nothing feels like trust. Context is the discipline of staying in the middle when either extreme is easier.

When More Context Is Needed

Not every task needs the full four parts. Telling a senior engineer to fix a bug in the area they have owned for three years does not require the why, the win, the boundaries, and the how. They know all of it. Over-contexting routine work wastes everyone's time.

The four parts earn their cost when one of these is true:

- **The work crosses teams.** Handoffs are where the boundaries live, and they are the part most often missed when you are working inside your own group.

- **The person is new.** New to the team, the company, or the kind of problem. They do not yet have the picture you have built from meetings they were not in.

- **The stakes are bigger than the surface.** If the work requires choosing between competing goods, or if one deployment, one client email, one migration switch could do real damage, the team needs the context to weigh it.

- **You want judgment, not compliance.** Context is how you get the first. Clear instructions produce the second. If the situation might change while the work is underway, the team needs enough context to adapt without you.

Translate Through the Person

Half the work is shaping context to the task. The other half is shaping it to the person.

The same outcome changes shape depending on what you know about the person hearing it. The four parts stay constant; the weight each carries shifts.

Two engineers on the same team, same role, same target. One thrives when handed intent and turned loose. The other builds confidence from a map; handed the same intent with no guardrails, they spend the first week second-guessing whether they are solving the right problem. Same sentence, *every workload in the new environment by March*, plays differently in two different minds. For the first, the *how* is the part to emphasize: here is the win, here is the boundary, now choose the route. For the second, the *why* and the *boundaries* carry more weight. They can decide; they decide better when the guardrails are drawn clearly.

Both get the full four parts. Each gets them in the form they can use.

This is where the Truth Ladder and context meet. Each rung of the Ladder shapes a different part of context.

Level 2 (range) tells you whether the *how* can be wide or has to come drawn on a map. Level 3 (drive) shapes which part of context carries the most weight, because people commit differently to a *why* that matches what they are working toward.

Level 4 (horizon) tells you which parts of the work a person will volunteer for when you leave the *how* open. Level 5 (fears) tells you what context the person will not hear until a specific concern is addressed. Take the new hire who cannot act on the *win* until the *boundaries* reassure them they will not be blamed for making the wrong call.

Context without Ladder knowledge reaches the team as a memo. Ladder knowledge without context is care without direction. Put them together and the same outcome compels the engineer who wants mastery, the product lead who wants impact, and the new hire who wants not to look foolish in front of the senior team. Each hears a version of the sentence that meets them where they are.

The same sentence also carries different risk. A principal hears *every workload in the new environment by March* as a problem to shape. A new hire, still proving they belong, hears the same sentence as a test they cannot afford to fail. When you deliver context to someone whose footing is newer, spend more on the *how*: name what is safely theirs to decide. They will not spend the first week solving for your approval instead of the problem.

The Questions I Check Myself On

Three questions do most of the work for me when I want to test whether I have translated strategy clearly enough for my team.

1. **What are our team's strategic goals?** The measurable outcomes we are responsible for. If I cannot name them in a sentence, the team will not either.

2. **How does our team's work connect to the organization's strategy?** Not metaphorically. Literally. A line upward through the hierarchy.

3. **What should we say no to?** What is outside our strategic focus, and how do we handle requests that fall outside it.

If I cannot answer one of these cleanly, I need to go back upstream for more context before I try to hand anything down. If my team can answer them, they do not need me hovering over their shoulders. They have what they need to make decisions without me, prioritize their own work, and push for what the work requires.

Make Them Decide

Context is what makes delegated judgment possible. Giving it and then taking the decisions back is the quickest way to prove the context was theater.

The default response when a direct report brings you a problem should be a question: *what do you think we should do?* Most of what slows organizations down is not the difficulty of decisions. It is the queue of decisions sitting several levels above the work, waiting for a signature that carries no new information.

When the decision is bigger than one person, when a room is evaluating an idea together, give them the structure to do it without anyone having to attack or defend. Four questions, in order: *Benefit* (what do we gain? — the upside and who gets it), *Enablers* (who do we need? — input, approval, expertise; a long list is its own signal), *Blockers* (what is in the way? — cost, time, technical debt, the ongoing weight of success), *Risk* (what if we fail? — blast radius, what is lost).

Take notes through all four together. If the picture is clear by the end, decide. If it needs more research or another conversation, defer; that is discipline, not indecision. Either way, the team examined the idea, not the person who proposed it.

When the team gets a decision wrong, and they will sometimes, do not use the failure as an excuse to take decisions back. Debrief, identify what they missed, and let them try again with more information. Taking decisions away after a miss teaches the team that you did not actually trust them. You were waiting for an excuse to step in. The trust breaks, and it does not come back easily.

The sentence you write for the team reaches each person through what you know of them. They reach the target through what they know of each other.

Three Ideas to Carry

- **Specify the what; trust the how.** The most useful thing a manager hands a team is one sentence the team can recite back. Write less, more carefully.

- **Context is the discipline of staying in the middle.** Control and abdication are both easier: one micromanages the decisions, the other surrenders them. Context keeps the decision with the person doing the work and equips them to make it well.

- **Context without Ladder knowledge reaches the team as a memo. Ladder knowledge without context is care without direction.** The same outcome changes shape through what you know about each person; the translation is what makes the sentence reachable instead of just heard.

In This Chapter

The Trust That Doesn't Pass Through You

12

> *"No member of a crew is praised for the rugged individuality of his rowing."*
>
> — Ralph Waldo Emerson

Managing the people on your team is half the job. The other half is managing what happens between them.

"They were all stars."

THE strength of a team is not only how much each person trusts you. It is also how much they trust each other. Part II was about one person at a time — the weekly one-on-one, what drives them, the work that grows them. That work is the spine of the job, but it isn't the whole of it. A team is not a set of one-on-one relationships the manager holds together. It is a web. If two of your engineers do not trust each other, the work grinds no matter how good your coaching is. Information gets hoarded. Code reviews turn into turf wars. Decisions get routed up to you because the peers will not align.

The last chapter was about clarity the team can carry. This one is about the strands they carry it on: the horizontal trust between the people on the team. That trust does not pass through you at all, but when it is missing, you become the permanent middleman. You are the human router for every decision, every clarification, every fragile handoff. At first you feel in control. Eventually it becomes drag.

The work of the web is three moves: predict friction before it forms, refuse to be the node every message has to pass through, and design the seams where work crosses between people. The gradient runs between peers too, in quieter forms (Chapter 2). Each of those three moves is the same work turned sideways, so a hard message can travel directly between two of your reports without routing through you.

Before any of those three moves matters, the web has to be composed in the first place. The hires you make and inherit are the first decisions of building it.

Who You Hire Reshapes the Web

The web you manage is the one you have helped assemble. Every hire reshapes it. Adding one person changes how the others connect and depend on each other. The hiring brief that gets written down names the title and the skills. The brief that actually matters, the one nobody writes, is about the team you have: which strand this hire reinforces, which connection is too thin, which disagreement the team doesn't currently know how to have.

Three patterns to watch.

Hiring in your own image. When the people you say *yes* to all share your way of working, the team gets faster in narrow ways and brittler in others. Imagine three engineers who all default to ship-fast-iterate; the first time the work calls for the careful one, nobody has the instinct. A homogeneous web has fewer routes for disagreement, and disagreement is the muscle the team uses when reality contradicts the assumptions that hired everyone in the first place.

Hiring for the immediate gap without checking the pair. A senior hire who could carry the work alone may collide with the principal already on the team if both want to own it. Before the offer goes out, walk the pairing forward in your head: who on the team will this person work with most often, and what will that pairing teach the rest of the team about who is allowed in which room?

Hiring senior when the team has not made space for it. Bringing in a seasoned hire above an existing senior who did not get the promotion is a structural decision, not a hiring decision. The existing senior is paying for it, and they are deciding right now whether to grow into the new structure or to start interviewing. A version of this conversation belongs in their one-on-one before the new hire signs, not after.

The team reads every hire as a statement about who belongs here. The brief is about the team you are building one strand at a time.

Reading the Ladder Sideways

Chapter 1 introduced the Truth Ladder as a way to map each person on your team. The natural way to read the Ladder is one person at a time, climbing higher. It also runs sideways, because the first strands of the web are pairs. The rungs that travel sideways are mostly the lower ones: what each peer can do (Range) and what motivates them (Drive). Peers rarely need to know each other's Horizon or Fears.

> *What each pair of people on your team knows about each other predicts where the dependence between them is going to create friction.*

When you pair two people on a project, what matters most is that each person's strengths, gaps, and motivations show up. You do not need peers to know each other's fears. You need to know each of them well enough to see the friction coming before they do. If you do not, the pair will read that friction as a character flaw when the real cause was a mismatch you could have named for them.

Pair an engineer whose motivation is deep, uninterrupted mastery with a product manager whose motivation is high-energy collaboration. The engineer wants to disappear into the problem for three days and come out with a clean design. The PM wants a ten-minute sync every afternoon to feel the progress. Within a week, the engineer has decided the PM is a micromanager who will not let them work. The PM has decided the engineer is evasive and uncooperative. Both come to you and complain about the other. Neither is wrong about what they observed. Both are wrong about what caused it.

Where the work allows, put people together whose styles line up or complement each other cleanly. Where the styles will collide anyway, name the difference out loud before the project starts. *"Sarah, you move fast and iterate. David, you want the foundation solid before you ship. You may frustrate each other in the first few days. Here is how I want you to split the decision-making so it does not become personal."*

Peers do not decode each other's strengths and motivations on their own. You already know the team at that level. Map the gaps for them, and a lot of the friction you would have been coaching through later never forms.

The practical move is two short conversations you have in the hallway or at the top of a project kickoff. To the engineer, while walking out of a one-on-one: *"Sarah's best when she has something rough to pull apart. If you bring her the polished version, she won't know where to help. Send her the ugly draft.*" To Sarah, the same day: "*David does his strongest thinking alone. If you ask him to sync three times a week he'll miss what he's actually good at. Ask him for a decision memo on Friday and trust the silence in between.*" You are pre-loading the moves they would have had to learn from friction. The two peers carry the map forward themselves after that.

Pairs also carry their own gradient. Seniority, tenure, the peer who has the relationship with the manager, the one who speaks in the style that gets rewarded in meetings: each tilts a pair without anyone naming it. A junior engineer paired with a principal will file her concerns through a gradient she does not name and the principal does not feel. The manager who treats a pair as symmetric when it is not will read the quiet end of it as agreement.

Name the Pattern Early

Not every tear in the web comes from a mismatched pair. Some come from patterns that have already formed inside an existing team: habits people have learned to work around instead of name. Before a dynamic hardens into something the team will carry for years, there is usually a window where naming the pattern out loud is enough.

I had a senior engineer named Victor whose default in team meetings was to explain why any idea would not work. If someone brought a proposal, his first move was to find the flaw. If he could not find one, he would say he had no specific reason but he believed the idea was wrong, and he would offer to run it just to watch it fail. Sometimes he had a better alternative and wanted to steer the group there. More often he just wanted to steer. People stopped bringing ideas to those meetings. The meetings got quieter. The team stopped generating options, which is how you know the web is starting to fray.

I waited longer than I should have. The junior engineers had started preempting their own suggestions. They would preface an idea with "*this probably won't work, but...*" because they had learned that Victor's first move was to find the reason. That is the tell. When people start writing the rebuttal into their own idea before they present it, the network is already hurt.

I brought it up in a one-on-one. I told Victor that I assumed his intent was good: he did not want the team to ship something bad, and his technical standards were part of why the team had a bar at all. Then I told him his effect on the team had stopped matching his intent. He was the most senior voice in the room, and people were calibrating their own contributions to what they expected him to do with them. If he kept playing the role of the filter, the team would stop generating the things he was supposed to filter. I asked him to let an idea breathe for a minute before he tested it, and to notice how often his testing had a real objection behind it and how often it was a reflex.

He took it harder than I expected, and also took it seriously. But rather than leave the change to willpower, I paired him with Nadia, one of the junior engineers on the team, and asked him to be her mentor. I told him I wanted him to be the great mentor I knew he could be, honest in a way that was humane. The standards could stay. What I wanted him to practice was the delivery. Standing next to someone while they worked through their own thinking, and holding his feedback in a way the other person could use.

I watched the relationship develop through the next few projects. Victor took it seriously. Nadia grew visibly. The two of them started bringing joint proposals into team meetings, and something about seeing Victor present *with* someone instead of *at* them changed the dynamics. A few projects in, I told him about the next step. I said the way he was showing up with Nadia was the way I wanted him to show up with everyone on the team. The behavior was already there. He had been practicing it for a while. What was left was to carry it into the meetings where it was harder.

The meetings got much more productive. The team started bringing ideas again. The whole shift took months, and mostly held.

What made the intervention work was the sentence *"your effect has stopped matching your intent."* That gave Victor a feedback loop he could adjust. If I had told him he was negative, he would have spent the next three months defending the verdict instead of changing. The pairing with Nadia did more than give him a place to practice. In team meetings, Victor was also defending his seniority: catching the flaw was how he proved he was the sharpest person in the room. With Nadia, he had nothing to prove. The skill underneath could come through, and the generalization came last.

A few months later, a new senior engineer joined the team. I started noticing Victor pushing back again in meetings, testing ideas a little too quickly. I watched for a few weeks and realized he was doing it because he felt challenged. The new engineer was technically strong and comfortable presenting. Victor was not the obvious senior voice in the room anymore, and the old habit came back when his status felt uncertain. We had another conversation. The pattern eased. I learned that this kind of change does not stay fixed on its own — it needs watching for years, not months.

Bringing In a New Member

A new hire's first ninety days look, from inside the manager's calendar, like a sequence of one-on-ones, an onboarding plan, and a handful of handoffs. From inside the team, they look like the formation of a new strand. Where it attaches first decides what kind of strand it becomes.

Most onboarding plans focus on what the new person needs to learn. The plan that matters more is who they meet first, and in what order. The peer you sit them with for week one is the peer whose habits they will absorb and through whose eyes they will read the rest of the team for the first month. A new engineer paired for their first project with a peer whose default is to share half-formed thinking will learn that the team works that way; paired with a peer who only ships finished work, they will spend the next two years trying to unlearn it. Pick the peer whose working style you would want repeated, not the one whose calendar happens to be open.

Watch for the first pushback. The new hire who has spent eight weeks careful, watching, agreeing, and then in the ninth week disagrees with a decision in a team meeting, is showing you something the rest of the time has not. They have decided the meeting is safe enough to be wrong in. Curiosity strengthens the strand they are forming. Correction or condescension teaches them the careful version was the right read all along. Most of the calibrations a new member makes about the team are made in the early days, and most are silent.

The Solo Star

Some threats to the network are people, not misreads.

Soren was technically exceptional. He could solve anything thrown at him, and the work was always high quality. But he never asked for help, never explained how he solved a problem, and deflected every request to share what he knew. Sometimes when I assigned a task to a newer team member so they could learn by doing, Soren jumped in and did it before the junior had a chance to start. When I asked for documentation, there was always an urgency that took priority. The work he produced was sophisticated but opaque, difficult for anyone else to maintain or build on.

Week by week, Soren was becoming indispensable, and that was the problem. He was a domain expert in an area the team depended on, and he was making sure nobody else could operate in that space. The team's capability was shrinking as his output grew. By the time I recognized the pattern clearly, unwinding it took months of cross-training, pairing sessions, documentation sprints. He resisted every step. From his point of view, he was losing time to teammates who should have known the material already, and teaching them was not his job. His individual output looked like a 10x contribution. The effect on the team was the opposite.

In a hub-and-spoke model, Soren looked like a star. His tasks shipped on time and the code was solid. Outside our team he was universally admired. If you asked any team we worked with, they would have named him our strongest member.

In the network we depended on, the same person was a choke point. Everything in his area routed through him. Nothing he learned made it back out. The junior engineers stopped asking him questions. The senior peers stopped pushing back in design reviews because the exchange was not worth it. The team's collective ability to operate in that area was decaying at the same speed his individual output was accelerating, and nobody outside the team could see it happening.

The solo star is not a passive bottleneck or a personality flaw. Each act of withholding, the doc that does not get written, the pairing that does not happen, the answer given without the reasoning, severs a strand of horizontal trust that would otherwise have formed. The web shrinks because their success depends on no one else learning the work.

This is a test of peer trust, and a test for you. Your people are watching what behavior gets rewarded. If you tolerate the solo star because the individual output is high, the team concludes that your speeches about culture are theater and that the standards only apply to the people who are not talented enough to break them.

So you confront the behavior. The first conversation is a flat naming of the pattern, with no preamble that softens the observation away. *"I want to be direct. The work you ship is genuinely better than what most of the team can produce right now. The team's collective ability in your area is also shrinking week over week. Both are real, and I cannot let the second one keep being true."* Pause there. Let them respond. The pattern they have been operating inside has felt invisible from where they sit; the first conversation is mostly about making it visible.

Then the new bar, named concretely. *"Making the people around you better is now part of how this job is done. That means a weekly pairing session, a documentation write-up the team can use, and walking two peers through your last technical decision. These are the new floor for how this part of the work gets done."* Being the best person in an area right now does not mean being the only person allowed in it forever. Teach it. Pair on it. Let the knowledge move.

If the bar is refused, if the pairing becomes a performance, the doc never gets written, the review becomes a monologue, the conversation has one more move. *"I gave you the new bar weeks ago. The pairing has not happened, the doc has not been written, the review became a monologue. I am not going to keep negotiating with you about whether the team gets to operate in this area. We will move you off the team. I am telling you now so you have time to decide what you want to do with the next conversation."* The short-term pain of losing a strong individual contributor is real. On the week they leave, you will watch the rest of the team exhale, step into the space, and start producing at a level the solo star was never going to allow.

Refuse to Triangulate

Choke points form around conflict too, when every hard message gets routed through you.

Sooner or later an employee will sit down in a one-on-one and start complaining about a peer. They are dropping the ball. They talked over you in a meeting. They ignored your message yesterday. Your instinct, if you care about the person in front of you, will be to be helpful. You listen, you validate their frustration, and you say: *"Let me talk to them and sort this out."*

That sentence is the trap.

By taking the message from one peer to another, you stripped the first one of their agency and denied the second a chance to hear the complaint from the person who actually has it. You also taught the whole team a rule. Friction here is something you bring to the manager, not something you work out at the desk where it lives. Once your team believes that, you will spend the rest of the job playing a game of telephone, and every unresolved peer conflict will be sitting on your calendar instead of being worked out between the people who own it. That is triangulation, and it is one of the easiest ways a well-meaning manager destroys their team's ability to self-repair.

When someone brings a peer conflict to your one-on-one, your first response is a question. *"Have you talked to them directly about this?"*

If the answer is no, your job is to coach the conversation, not to have it for them. The coaching is a short sequence. First, separate what they saw from what they concluded. *"You said she undercut you in the meeting. What did she actually do? What did she say?"* Get them to the behavior, not the verdict. Second, name the impact. What did the behavior cost them, or the team, or the work? That is what they will lead with in the real conversation, and it is what the other person can actually respond to. Third, hand them an opening sentence they could say out loud. *"In yesterday's review you cut me off twice. I wanted to finish the point about the caching approach, and I did not get to. Can we talk about that?"* Let them rework it in their own voice.

Then draw the line: *"I need you to tell them what you just told me. I will sit in the room with you if you want me there. I will not carry the message for you."* That sentence closes the shortcut you would otherwise take.

There are exceptions. The rule is for ordinary peer friction like missed handoffs, irritating meeting behavior, the slow accumulation of small grievances that two adults can work out between them if you give them the structure to try. The rule does not apply when the issue is harassment or bullying, when there is a sharp power imbalance between the two people, when there is a real risk of retaliation, or when the person in front of you has already tried a direct conversation and been shut down. In those cases, carrying the message yourself, or intervening directly, is exactly the job. Know the difference and act.

The first few times you do this, you may feel like you are failing them. Try it anyway. A team where two adults cannot give each other hard feedback without a manager present will break the moment the manager is not there.

Designing Handoffs

Handoffs are the places where trust between peers is built or torn.

Most team resentment hides inside a bad one. The first person felt finished; the second opens the work and finds missing context, decisions made without them, unanswered questions at the edges. Neither complains out loud. The frontend engineer starts over-reviewing the designer's files. The designer feels micromanaged. The engineer makes scope decisions without telling the project manager. The project manager finds out from the customer. Each side invents character flaws for the other to explain what the process should have made explicit.

The way out is to stop coaching the tone and start designing the seam.

When work moves from one person to another, five things should be clear:

- **What is done.** Specifically. What is finished, what is not.
- **What assumptions were made.** What did the first person believe to be true when they made the calls they made?
- **What quality bar was used.** Rough draft, decision-ready recommendation, or ready to ship?
- **What risks remain.** What still looks uncertain, fragile, or under-tested?
- **Who owns the next move.** Ambiguity about ownership is usually the real failure of a handoff, not ambiguity about the past.

Do not write these rules yourself. Put the two people in a room and ask them to write the standard down together. *"When work passes from you to them, what does a perfect handoff look like?"* When the contract is in their own words, peers stop judging each other's intentions and start evaluating the work against the thing they both agreed to.

I learned this on a cross-functional project where engineering and product kept blaming each other. Product felt engineering was resistant and late; engineering felt product was vague and constantly changing direction. Both were partly right; the real issue was that the handoff between them was undefined. Once we named what had to be true before engineering could start, what decisions had to be documented, and what was still legitimately open, most of the "chemistry problem" disappeared. Most problems that look like personality are problems of inattention to the seams.

What the Team Believes

A team's character is the sum of who is on it, the disciplines the manager has practiced visibly, and the rituals the team has chosen to keep. None of it is written down, and all of it is obvious to anyone who has worked on the team for a quarter.

The first time the team handles a hard moment a particular way, that becomes the precedent. The second time, it becomes the pattern. By the third, it is the team's character, and any new member will read it as the way things are. If the pattern that hardened was not the one you would have chosen, the cost of changing it is roughly proportional to how long you let it set.

A few moves help. Name the norms out loud when the team is forming and again whenever someone joins: *we share rough drafts here; we disagree in the room, not after; we debrief our misses, we do not assign them.* Be explicit about what the team will not do: *we do not promise dates we have not stress-tested; we do not let one person carry a system that takes the team three months to learn.* Norms phrased as what the team won't do are easier to test than norms phrased as aspirations. And repeat the rituals across reorgs: the weekly demo, the debrief, the pattern of how a project gets launched. Rituals continued through the reorg are how the team's identity survives the org chart that no longer reflects it.

Build the Web

A manager who pays attention to what happens between people ends up with a team that can repair itself when they leave the room. One who does not ends up as the only person who can fix anything.

Three Ideas to Carry

- **A team is a web, not a set of one-on-one relationships.**
The horizontal trust is the part you do not pass through. If
two people on your team only ever resolve friction by routing
it through you, the team will break the moment you are not
in the room.

- **Read the Ladder sideways.** Range and Drive run between
peers as much as they do between manager and report; most
lateral friction is a misread at one of those rungs. Pre-load
the moves the pair would have learned from time together
they have not had yet.

- **Refuse to triangulate.** When a report brings you their friction with another report, your job is to coach the conversation,
not to have it for them. Carry the message and you teach the
team that hard things go through the manager.

In This Chapter

The Inheritors

*"Don't ever take a fence down until you
know the reason why it was put up."*

— G.K. Chesterton

*The people who approve the work are not always the people who
inherit it.*

K NOWING the people on your team is the foundation; knowing
whose work crosses theirs is the next ring out. Before the
work starts, ask one question: *who inherits this?* Not who
approved it. Who lives with it after delivery, two years from now, at
3am when it breaks.

Each part of the context frame from Chapter 11 has an owner —
and the owners are rarely the same person. The four parts are the *why*
(the reason), the *win* (what success looks like), the *how* (the team's
decision space), and the *boundaries* (what it must not violate). The
gradient from Chapter 2 runs between teams, too: a constraint held
by someone outside the project's inner circle reaches you later than
one held by someone inside it. You can get clean sign-off from one of
them and still fail delivery. I learned this on a project that went well
until the moment it was handed over.

A Sign-Off That Wasn't

Years ago I led a small team building a cloud-management application for a customer. The build ran six to eight weeks. Every two weeks we demoed progress to a group that included the customer's VP, and we kept those demos at a business-value altitude: features tied to outcomes the VP's organization cared about. Every sign-off came through cleanly. We shipped on schedule, wrote the manuals, and handed the application to the customer's operations team.

Their operations team ran their production applications in Python. All of them. Their runtime, their monitoring, their on-call playbooks assumed Python. We had built ours in TypeScript.[1]

At first I thought the customer had changed what they wanted. The customer-contact I had been working with had told us, directly, that there was no language preference. We had asked. We had been told. Someone else was changing the rules after the fact.

Then I sat with it for an hour and saw what I had done.

The customer-contact who told us "no language preference" was the business owner — the person who wanted the application to exist. He had given us permission. He had not given us the constraint. The constraint lived with the operations team, a separate customer-side stakeholder we had never asked, because the demos had always been with the VP and the business owner. The *win* was well-defined. The *why* was in place. The team had the *how* — the latitude to pick the stack. The *boundary* — what "production ready" meant in the environment that would actually run the code — was the part nobody had surfaced. By the time it mattered, we had six weeks of TypeScript.

We rewrote it in Python in two weeks. The rewrite was not hard — we had a good understanding of the logic and had mapped the edge cases. We just had to solve it again in a different language.

I felt stupid. I had been demoing the wrong success.

Every demo had shown the VP the business value his organization had asked for, and I had taken those sign-offs as validation that the work was on track. They were validation of one part of the frame. The win. The boundaries lived in a room I never walked into.

Each Part Has an Owner

The failure has a pattern.

The sponsor owns the *why* and the *win*, the outcome they need and the success they will measure. They are also the ones the project is organized around, which puts them at the center of every kickoff and status review.

The *inheritors* own the *boundaries*. The people who will live with the work after delivery. Most of their constraints do not announce themselves until the work reaches their hands.

The team owns the *how*.

Treat sign-off from the sponsor as sign-off on all four parts, and you can pass every gate and still fail delivery. The business owner in my story had the authority to approve what we were building. He did not have the authority to tell us what "production ready" meant on a runtime his team did not operate. Nobody was lying. Each person in the meeting had the parts of the frame they owned. The rest of the frame lived in a meeting we had never scheduled.

This is the default whenever the people who request work and the people who inherit it are not the same.

Ask Who Inherits It

The practical move is a single page written before scoping. Two columns: the four parts in one, the owner in the other. The *why* goes next to the sponsor. The *win* goes next to whoever defines what success looks like. The *boundaries* get broken out. Runtime to operations. Compliance envelope to legal or security. Downstream contracts to consuming teams. The *how* goes to the team.

When a row in the owner column is blank, you know where the next conversation is. When a row has more than one name, you know where the next disagreement is going to come from.

> *A boundary that nobody surfaced is a boundary that will surface late.*

Most of the time those conversations are short and produce a constraint nobody had in writing. Occasionally they produce one big enough that the project changes scope before it starts.

Outside Tech

The same pattern shows up outside tech. Mira manages a store at a regional retail chain. Corporate's loyalty-app push is in its third week. The cashiers have been trained, the design has been signed off, the store managers were sent the launch deck. On a busy afternoon, Mira watches a line back up and realizes the app is the reason.

To enroll a customer, the cashier reads the phone-number prompt aloud across the counter, because the registers at her store do not have customer-facing screens. The customer reads the number back. The cashier confirms by reading it again, over the ambient noise of the floor. On a quiet morning it adds thirty seconds per transaction. At peak, it is the difference between three lines and seven.

The app team at corporate had approved the design. Mira's cashiers and her shoppers inherited the friction. Nobody in the app-selection meetings had asked which stores had customer-facing screens at checkout and which did not. The constraint belonged to the physical layout of her store — a fact Mira could have named in twenty seconds. She wasn't in those meetings.

Mira's cashiers were the operators in that rollout, running the loyalty-app at the register every day. Hers is the easy version. Most missed inheritors are harder to spot.

Who Most Often Gets Missed

Some inheritors are easy to see like the immediate downstream team, the customer named in the brief, the senior manager who signs the expense report. Others sit further from the discussion where scope gets decided, and they hold some of the most unforgiving constraints.

The operators. The people who run the system day to day. They hold the boundaries of operational reality: how it behaves under load, what breaks at 3am, what the on-call rotation can absorb. They get missed when their work is going well, which is most of the time.

The supporters. The people who get paged when it fails and explain it to customers while it is failing. They hold the boundaries of failure cost: reputational and relational as much as technical. They get missed when they sit downstream of two or three other teams.

The maintainers. The people who inherit the code, the process, the runbook two years from now, after the original team has moved on. What they pay for is undocumented decisions: the choice nobody wrote down, the constraint nobody named, the workaround that became load-bearing. They get missed when they don't yet exist at the time of the decision.

The consumers. The downstream teams whose own work depends on this one's output. They live with the structure of your data, your release cadence, your reliability. They get missed when the project is organized around producing something, not around who will consume it.

The reviewers. Compliance, legal, security, procurement. They hold the boundaries the project cannot negotiate: regulatory, contractual, organizational. They get missed when engaging them feels expensive, which is exactly the moment engagement is cheapest.

None of them hide. They are knowable, and most of their constraints are predictable. They get missed because the project's center of gravity is somewhere else, and they sit further from it than the requester does.

The gradient from Chapter 2 runs here too, in a different key. A constraint held by someone with less project-politics power has farther to travel before it gets heard. The operations team in my story was not absent from the work; they were absent *from the discussions where this got decided*, and the absence was structural rather than neutral. When the frame finally met reality, the constraints the project had made easy to hear had been heard on time, and the ones it had made hard to hear had been heard late.

Late constraints are often treated as late objections. Many are not. They are early truths that came late because they had farther to travel.

Your job is to go get them. Ask who the work will reach. Ask the inheritors what they need before the requester finishes telling you what they want. If you only consult the people the project has made easy to reach, you will miss the constraints held by everyone else.

Repairing After a Missed Inheritor

The inheritor question is cheapest to ask early. It can also be asked late, when a project is struggling. There are two repairs, and finishing the first does not finish the second. The retrofit fixes the project. The relationship with the inheritor you missed is a separate repair, and slower.

Pull the project back to the four parts. The *why* — does the team and the requester still describe the same reason for this work, or has one drifted toward compliance while the other still hears revenue? The *win* — when you ask each side what success looks like, do they describe the same thing, or does one say "shipped on schedule" and the other say "adoption hit forty percent"? The *boundaries* — what has the team been discovering in the last few weeks that nobody had scoped for? The *how* — is the team's decision space the one it was supposed to be, or has it narrowed under them?

Trouble usually surfaces at the boundaries, a constraint that was true all along but nobody in the early discussions named it. The retrospective question is whose constraint that was, and why they were not in the meeting when the scope got decided.

Name it with the team, then with them. A team that discovers a constraint late needs to hear you say what happened, plainly, before they do the repair. Otherwise the team treats the rewrite as random cost and looks for whose failure it was. *"We scoped this without the operations team. I should have had them in the scoping meeting. We have two weeks of work to undo because I did not."* Said once, with the team, the rewrite stops being a mystery and becomes a fix. Then have the same conversation with the missed inheritor before you walk in asking what they need.

Ask what else you're about to miss. The inheritor you just surfaced has been holding more than one constraint. Ask before you scope the fix: *what else would you have told us if we had asked three months ago?* The answer usually includes things that have nothing to do with the current miss and would have hit you later. One late conversation can prevent two.

Triage the retrofit. Not every discovered constraint is worth a rewrite. Some can be met by documentation, a runbook, or a wrapper that fits the inheritor's tooling. In our case the rewrite was the right call. The alternative we did not seriously consider was wrapping the TypeScript service so the operations team could drive it from their Python stack; by the time we weighed it, the rewrite was already faster. Decide which constraints cost enough late to be worth paying for early. The rest go on the owner page as known constraints, not ignored ones.

Pay the cost visibly. If the retrofit is two weeks, budget the two weeks and say so. A project plan that stopped telling the truth in week four is a project that will stop being trusted in every week after.

The page nobody wrote at kickoff gets written now. The list of inheritors, with what they own, and which parts of the frame need their sign-off before the project can move again.

The retrofit is what lets the project ship. The relationship is the slower repair. The operations team in my story did not say, in so many words, that they had been disrespected. They did not have to. We had built a thing on their ground without asking them what the ground was, and then we had asked them to run it. The Python rewrite was not the repair; the repair was whether their next project with us started with them at the table. Three moves shape that conversation.

Lead with what you got wrong about their world, not their constraint. Their constraint was that they ran Python. That is the surface. The underlying thing you missed was their world. The on-call load, the runbook library, the way a new language would have rippled across their tooling. When you sit down with them afterward, do not lead with *"we should have asked what stack you used."* Lead with *"I did not sit with your on-call before I committed to a stack. I did not know what the Python tooling had cost you to build, and I did not ask."* The first sentence treats it as a process miss. The second treats it as a failure of respect. It was the second.

Don't promise it won't happen again. You cannot guarantee that. What you can do is change the structure that let it happen. Propose one: the next scoping meeting includes an inheritor-ask, or the requester's sign-off is paired with an operations sign-off, or the owner page is written before the project is greenlit. Something structural and checkable, not a personal promise you will not keep when the next project is in a rush.

Don't make them the gatekeeper. The instinct after missing an inheritor is to involve them in every decision going forward. That load is worse than the miss. They did not sign up to review your team's choices. The move is to make inheritor-surfacing part of your process, so their presence is structural and selective — they get called in on the decisions that need them, and left alone on the ones that do not.

Some relationships do not repair. Sometimes the inheritor has seen this pattern too many times, or the miss was too expensive, or your leverage to change the structure is smaller than you think. In that case the work is to be honest about it with your team. Treat the pattern as information about the organization. This place has a seam between requesters and inheritors, and you will keep paying for it as long as you work here.

When the Inheritor Was Kept Out on Purpose

Sometimes the missed inheritor was not missed by accident. They were kept out of the meeting because the project had a reason: they block too much, they slow everything down, they will say no to something the business has decided it needs. When the reason is real, the question is not how to sneak past them. It is how to engage them on the specific constraint without re-litigating the scope.

Distinguish between two things they might hold. A *preference* is something they would like to see happen, shaped by their judgment. Preferences do not need sign-off. A *constraint* is a fact about their domain that will be true regardless of the project's preferences, like the regulatory clock, the runtime, the capacity of their team, the contracts they are already bound to. Constraints are not negotiable; they are surfaceable. Conflating the two is how a project swerves around a real constraint or stalls out over a preference.

When the inheritor holds a real constraint, engage on the constraint, not the scope. *"I am not asking you to approve the architecture. I am asking you for the two facts about your system that would change what we build."* That framing does not flatter the inheritor, but it respects the part of their authority that is not up for negotiation. They are more likely to give you the facts than the approval.

When the inheritor holds a veto over the project's scope and the business is proceeding anyway, escalate the tension before the project starts rather than hoping it will resolve. The organization is deciding, on the project's behalf, to overrule someone with authority. The project is not the right forum to litigate that decision. Your move is to make sure someone above you owns the override explicitly, so that when the inheritor surfaces the objection in week eight, they are surfacing it against the decision that was already made, not against your team's work.

When the inheritor has organizational power but no real constraint, your job is to keep them informed. Let them see the work at regular intervals. Objections raised early are cheaper than objections raised at delivery. A stakeholder who could have surfaced a concern in week two and only surfaces it in week twelve is, at that point, voicing a political position, not a constraint. The cadence prevents the twelve-week objection from being possible to make in good faith.

The worst version of this pattern is the inheritor who is kept out because the project assumes their constraint is immovable. The project proceeds as if the constraint does not exist, hoping the inheritor will move when delivery is close. They usually do not. The constraint hits the project at delivery instead, when moving it is hardest.

Context Also Runs Upward

The context frame you hand your team is partly built out of what the person above you carries. Their pressures, their commitments, the constraints they inherited from above. Asking the inheritors is half of the work. The other half is knowing the person above you well enough that their constraints reach your team before a hallway conversation does.

Three Ideas to Carry

- **Sign-off from the requester is not sign-off from the inheritor.** Each part of the frame has an owner; the owners are rarely the same person. You can pass every gate and still fail delivery.

- **A boundary that nobody surfaced is a boundary that will surface late.** Late constraints are usually early truths that had a longer distance to travel. The fix is not to discount them on arrival; it is to shorten the distance next time.

- **Lead with what you got wrong about their world, not their constraint.** The retrofit fixes the project. The relationship is a slower repair, and it starts with showing the inheritor you know what was on their side of the line.

In This Chapter

The Truth Ladder Runs Upward

Learn What They Actually Care About

Surface Bad News Early

Push Back Without Breaking the Relationship

When the Ladder Hits a Wall

Am I the Problem?

The Relationship That Shapes the Ceiling

Three Ideas to Carry

The Truth Ladder Runs Upward

Know your manager the way you know your team.

"He was the last to know he was the bottleneck."

M Y manager brought it to me in a one-on-one. A customer was unhappy with the delivery velocity on one of our teams. The complaint had traveled the full chain before it reached me. Customer to his boss, his boss to him, him to me. The team was too slow. The customer wanted more, faster.

But the complaint did not match what I was seeing. Several people were already staying late. The problem was not effort. The dependencies were real, the testing had to be coordinated across systems, and the requirements kept shifting as the customer learned more about their own problem. The target moved, and the team chased it.

I told the customer what I was seeing. They did not disagree. They still wanted the original date.

I brought it back to my manager. He was caught between promises already made and the reality I was describing, and he chose optimism. If we pushed harder, he thought, we could close the gap. I knew the team was already past their hours. I said so, but not hard enough. Instead I rolled up my sleeves and tried to help directly: reviewing designs, unblocking dependencies, sitting in on calls I would normally have skipped.

It did not work. The customer's dissatisfaction grew because the pace did not change. My leadership heard the same complaint again. The team eventually learned the customer had been unhappy for weeks, and they felt two things at once. Frustration that nobody had told them, and confusion about why I had been hovering over their work when they thought they were doing fine. The shielding I meant as fairness was experienced as withholding.

What I owed my manager was a second conversation, firmer than the first. I never had it.

That year taught me something simple. Managing up is the same work you do with your team, applied in the other direction. The person above you has a range, drives, pressures, and fears of their own, and most of what you have been reading as character flaws are patterns you can learn to read.

The asymmetry runs upward here. In Chapter 2 the gradient ran downward, and your people talked to you through risk. Here you are the one talking through risk. The reflexes that make you fold with your manager are the same reflexes your own reports use with you.

You cannot do this book's work if the relationship above you is broken. When it works, your team gets resources, your decisions get backed, and you earn freedom to act without asking permission for every move. When it does not, you spend your energy managing around the gap instead of managing your people.

The Truth Ladder Runs Upward

The Truth Ladder works upward too. One rung changes name.

Level 1: Role. You know your boss's title, reporting line, and meetings. If you stop here, you manage a title, not a person.

Level 2: Range. You know what they are good at, where they add value, and where they struggle. Strategy but not follow-through. Data but not people. People but not systems. This tells you where they need help, whether they ask for it or not.

Level 3: Drive. You know what moves them. Operational excellence. Team development. Visibility. Precision. Stability. The same request will read differently to each of them depending on which drive it touches.

Level 4: Pressures. This is the upward equivalent of Horizon. What is their boss asking about? What problem are they carrying that you rarely see? Understand the pressure, and you stop being surprised by half their decisions.

Level 5: Fears. The reaction that is bigger than the moment. The defensiveness. The control. The avoidance. You do not get here by asking directly. You get here by watching patterns long enough to see what repeatedly trips the wire.

If you are managing up at Role only, you are delivering updates to a title. Reaching Drive and Pressures changes what you can accomplish.

Learn What They Actually Care About

Your boss has a stated priority list and a real one. They may not match.

The stated list lives in decks and quarterly goals. The real list reveals itself in what they ask about when nobody is presenting, like the question they repeat in one-on-ones, the thing they circle back to after meetings, the issue that seems to be on their mind even when the slide says something else.

One manager of mine kept asking the same kind of question. Had we informed a certain group about our progress? Had we pulled in the right adjacent team? Had we updated stakeholders outside our immediate lane? We didn't have a goal I could tie these questions back to.

I realized what he actually cared about. That our team's work be visible across the organization, and that we be connected to the people whose support we would eventually need. Once I saw that, I started doing more of it on purpose. Each connection helped the work on its own. Together they were a network we could draw on when support from outside the team mattered.

Before your next one-on-one, write down the three things you think your boss is most worried about right now. After the meeting, check yourself. Keep doing that for a month. You will know their real priority list far better than you do now.

The real list is only useful if you act on it before they ask. Before every interaction, ask yourself: *What is their boss asking them about right now?* Then frame your update in that language. You are not changing the substance of your work. You are translating it upward.

Surface Bad News Early

Telling your team bad news is uncomfortable. Telling your boss bad news can feel dangerous. It is still part of the job.

Most people delay upward bad news for familiar reasons. Maybe it will fix itself, maybe one more day will make the story cleaner, maybe I can solve it before I have to say it. Usually what we are protecting is ourselves.

Bad news gets more expensive with time. The later you surface it, the more it looks like concealment.

The formula:

- Name the problem clearly.
- Say what it means.
- Say what you need.

"The integration is two weeks behind because the external dependency has slipped again. If we keep the date, quality will drop. I need a decision today on whether we move the date, reduce scope, or add support."

That is a very different conversation from *"We're working through some issues."*

Bringing bad news early does not mean bringing it raw. Carry a recommendation. Your boss should not have to do their job and yours at the same time.

Push Back Without Breaking the Relationship

Managing up includes disagreement.

The worst version is silent disagreement followed by private work-arounds. The second-worst is disagreement that gets personal. The useful version is direct, specific, and bounded.

Name what you see. Explain the consequence. Offer an alternative.

"If we keep the original date, the team will absorb the pressure in hours and the quality risk will surface later. I think the better move is to cut scope and preserve the date, or keep scope and move the date. I do not think we can honestly do all three."

That is disagreement done well.

Once the decision is made, execute it fully. Do not keep relitigating it in side channels. Push back hard before the call. Align after it.

When the Ladder Hits a Wall

Everything so far assumes a boss you can climb the Ladder toward. Some people do not have that boss. The same diagnostic from Chapter 1 applies upward too.

The Ghost

If your boss is a ghost — vague on outcomes, shallow on you — you are manufacturing clarity from thin air. The four parts of context (why, win, boundaries, how) become your lifeline: supply them to your team, then propose them upward.

I worked for a ghost for a few years. I mistook absence for trust. It stopped working when I needed support above my level and nothing moved, and the team drifted because every direct report was building their own version of the priorities. I should have told him plainly that he was not doing the parts of the job only he could do. I accepted a ceiling I could have challenged.

Two tactical moves help. Force decisions onto paper with a clock: *"I am going to proceed with X unless I hear otherwise by Friday."* And send a weekly update they can skim in ninety seconds: what moved, what is blocked that needs them, what you will do if you hear nothing. Neither fixes the relationship but they keep the work moving while you decide what the ceiling means.

The Boss

If your boss is a boss — clear on outcomes, no real knowledge of you — you are receiving direction without relationship.

Request a regular one-on-one if you do not have one. Use it to teach them about your team, your constraints, and your thinking. In effect, you are climbing the Ladder for them.

Questions that help: *"Can I tell you about three people on my team you should know about?"* *"What is your boss asking about that I should be thinking about too?"* *"What is the most important thing the team should know next quarter that they don't know yet?"*

Two tactical moves help. Hand them one piece of context per one-on-one: a working detail about your team they could not have known otherwise, named in two sentences. And keep a running list of what they have asked twice; the second ask is usually a real priority you can preempt next time.

The Friend

If your boss is a friend — they know you well, but outcomes are vague — you have a good relationship with no structure underneath it.

Bring the structure yourself. Propose goals. Ask for explicit priorities. Get agreement in writing where you can.

There was a manager I genuinely liked and trusted. I could tell him about mistakes and doubts. What he did not give the team was signal from above or a clear filter on which work mattered most. I had a manager I could tell anything to, and nowhere that telling him would take me.

A one-page note before the next one-on-one can change that: *Here are the three things I think our team should focus on this quarter, in priority order. Do these match your view?*

Two tactical moves help. Convert warm verbal alignments into written form within a day — *"to make sure I have this right, here is what I heard"* — and watch which parts come back corrected; the corrections are the structure the friendship was hiding. And ask the question the relationship makes uncomfortable: *"If the team only ships one of these next quarter, which one?"* The friend's instinct is to say all of them. Force the choice anyway.

When It Is Worse Than Absent

Sometimes the person above you is damaging, not merely absent. A pattern of being diminished in rooms you are not in, used as a shield when things go wrong, credited late and blamed early. The managing-up practices in this chapter will not fix a relationship like that. They may buy time. They will not repair a person who is not trying to be a good manager.

Four moves form the protocol.

- **Documentation.** Keep a private record of incidents, dates, witnesses, and outcomes. Not as ammunition. As something solid when your version and theirs no longer agree.
- **Shielding the team.** Absorb what you can without lying about its source; tell people what is happening around them in the form they can act on, not the form that flatters you.
- **Escalation.** When the preconditions hold (concrete pattern, documented impact, a path through HR or a skip-level that will not retaliate), use them. Not before.
- **Decision deadline.** Set yourself a date by which you will choose to stay, leave, or change something material. Put it on a calendar. Sunk cost is not an argument for more months.

The Damaging Boss Protocol in the toolkit has the fuller sequence with thresholds and edge cases. The short version: a damaging relationship is rarely the team's secret to keep, and your endurance under it is not a virtue the organization will eventually reward.

Am I the Problem?

The four patterns are diagnostic for the boss above you. They are also a mirror.

If your reports are managing up to you, you are managing up to your own boss. The reflexes you read in your reports — the careful question, the smoothed update, the disagreement saved for the hallway — are reflexes you carry up the chain. The same gradient runs in both directions, and you are at the bottom of yours.

Ask yourself, on a project that is not going well: am I withholding the bad news because the framing is not ready, the same way my report withholds it from me? Am I sending updates that announce instead of inform? Am I treating the warmth of the relationship as a substitute for telling them something they need to know?

The honest answer is usually that you are doing one or two of them at any given time, and the question is which one is currently costing you the most.

The recovery is the same one you wish your reports would do. Surface what you have been holding. Trade the polished version for the rough one. Tell your boss what you are unsure about, not just what you have decided. The asymmetry is real on both sides; the only person who can soften it from below is you.

The Relationship That Shapes the Ceiling

The relationship above you sets the ceiling for the work you can do with and for your team.

Most upward relationships can be worked with. Learn what the person above you cares about, carry bad news early and with a recommendation, and disagree without going adversarial. A few relationships cannot be worked with, and staying under one for too long is its own cost.

Know the person above you the way you know the people below you, well enough to give them what they need and get what your team needs.

Three Ideas to Carry

- **The reflexes that make you fold with your manager are the same reflexes your reports use with you.** The asymmetry runs upward too, and the work of softening it is yours to do from below.

- **Push back hard before the call. Align after it.** Disagreement plus execution beats silent resistance. Side-channel relitigation is how trust dies on both sides.

- **Sunk cost is not an argument for more months.** Some upward relationships will not be repaired by the practices in this chapter. Set yourself a date and keep it.

PART IV

What You Carry

The first three parts are about what the manager does: knowing the people, shaping the work around them, helping the team carry context without you in every room. This final part is about what the work does to the manager—the pressure you absorb, the pressure you name, the pressure you refuse to pass down, and how to stay accurate while carrying it.

In This Chapter

Carry the Weight

> *"Hope is not the conviction that something will turn out well, but the certainty that something makes sense, regardless of how it turns out."*
>
> — Václav Havel

Every week, the manager decides what to absorb on behalf of the team and what to push back against.

"He said we'd be there by New Year."

MIDDLE management is a pressure-sorting job. Every team hits weather. The pressure is not the question. What you do with it is: week by week, what you carry and what you name.

Paying close attention has a cost. This chapter is for the hard weeks when you have to decide what belongs to you, what does not, and what is left of you after. It draws on the highest rung of the Truth Ladder, because when a team is under sustained pressure, the manager who has climbed there can see who is quietly drowning before they go under. The manager who only knows their roles cannot see it.

Leading Through Fatigue

Most resilience advice is designed for the kind of intensity that comes with a sprint or a launch. The more common challenge is quieter. It is a team worn down not from one thing but from everything.

Fatigue accumulates. One more quarter of stretch goals. Another reorganization. A key person leaves and the backfill takes months. The work keeps coming at the same pace, but the energy behind it drops. People still deliver but quality slips. Conversations in one-on-ones get shorter. Volunteers for new initiatives disappear. Nobody is complaining and nobody is quitting, but the team is running on less than it used to.

It does not show on everyone the same way. One person gets quieter and stops volunteering, another gets brittle when challenged, a third over-functions, taking on work that isn't theirs. The three questions from Chapter 6 catch what fatigue hides. Under fatigue, what is newly constrained? What has stopped stretching? What feels like it no longer matters?

This is harder to address than a crisis because there is nothing specific to fix. The weight itself is the problem, and naming it is the first move. *"I can see the team is tired. I feel it too."* Seconds to say. It tells people their experience is real and visible, not something they need to hide. Teams that never hear their fatigue acknowledged learn to treat exhaustion as a personal failure rather than a shared condition.

I faced this on a consulting engagement that ran for several months. The project was high-visibility, technically demanding, and a first for the customer. Our senior leaders visited on-site, took us to dinner with the customer. Everyone wanted it to succeed. The team flew out every Sunday, worked on-site Monday through Thursday, flew home Thursday night or Friday. Most of us were married. Some had kids. We started at eight or nine in the morning. After dinner, most of the team went back to the hotel meeting room and worked until midnight. We did this week after week.

The project was worth it. We were solving a real problem. But after several months, morale was eroding. People complained within the team. The energy that had carried the first few weeks was gone. It was getting to a point where people stopped being excited about the work itself, which was the clearest sign that something had to change. Nobody was about to quit. But the team was running on depleted reserves, and the difference between "people are tired" and "the work has stopped mattering to them" is where sustained projects live or die.

Going to my manager felt like the wrong conversation to have. The project was visible, the customer relationship was at a delicate stage, and asking leadership to slow down a strategic engagement was not a low-risk move. The shortcuts were tempting. I could have framed the change as customer-driven. I could have pushed the decision up the chain and left him out of it. Both would have bought short-term relief at the cost of the credibility I needed for every conversation with him that came after. The harder thing was to go through him and accept that the outcome would depend on whether I could make the case.

I told my manager, in person during one of his on-site visits, that the team could not continue traveling every week. It was unsustainable for the people, and eventually it would be unsustainable for the customer. He heard me out, but he couldn't bring himself to make the call. This was a critical engagement, and changing the cadence on it was not a decision he wanted to own alone. I talked to the customer separately and framed it in a way they could absorb. The question was not whether the project mattered, but whether the team that finished it would still be the team that started it. I talked to my leadership again. Everyone could see the problem. Nobody wanted to own the decision. So I forced the conversation. I told them I would not have the team on-site every week going forward, and that we needed to talk about what the new rhythm would look like.

That triggered the decision. We moved to every other week on-site, Monday through Thursday, with the understanding that travel would become ad-hoc at some point once the project stabilized. The team was relieved. I was not the only one who had been thinking it, but not everyone had the tenure to be that direct about it. That is the point. Some pressures require the person with the shortest distance to leadership to raise them, because nobody with a longer distance is going to take the risk. That is the asymmetry the leader is paid to absorb.

Naming the weight upward is one move. Inside the team, naming is not enough on its own. During sustained pressure, progress has to become visible. People can keep going for a long time when they can see movement; they start to break when effort disappears into the machine.[1] Small wins produce outsized energy; small losses drain motivation out of proportion to their size. The practical move during sustained difficulty is to break the work into milestones reachable in days, not months, and mark each one visibly — a brief acknowledgment in a team meeting, a message in Slack, a sentence in a one-on-one that names what moved and why. Without that, good work stops feeling like a win and starts feeling like what is expected.

> *Wait until the end to recognize progress and the team has carried the hardest part alone.*

I lived this on a difficult technical project. We were processing large volumes of data, and the method we had planned to use was proving unfeasible at scale. I built a proof of concept outside my primary responsibilities; the approach worked but was complicated, and standing behind it was risky because nothing about it had been tested at scale. I owned the risk. The team committed. Then it got harder than any of us had imagined. Integration was a maze. After every issue we solved, another appeared. The only way through was one problem at a time. I told the team the same thing every week: *this will not be easy, but it will work.* After months, it did. What kept the team moving was the small wins along the way. The eventual success was still far away.

The worst response to fatigue is to push harder and hope it passes. Usually it does not. It shows up later as turnover and quiet disengagement, and standards fall before anyone notices.

What Fatigue Hides Under Power

Fatigue does not look the same at every rung of the Ladder. At Level 1 (Roles), it shows up as missed tasks. At Level 2 (Range), as capacity strain — the work still ships, but at a quality bar lower than the person's range usually produces. At Level 3 (Drive), the work has stopped giving energy back; what used to feel like ownership now feels like throughput. At Level 4 (Horizon), someone is wondering whether this future is still worth wanting. At Level 5 (Fears), an old fear is back under the pressure — the conflict avoidance, the freeze at decisions, the vigilance that does not quite turn off at night. A manager who knows only the work sees the miss. A manager who knows the person sees the load.

The manager who has reached the highest rung sees who is quietly drowning — sometimes. Under asymmetry, drowning is hidden hardest by the people closest to going under. They cannot afford to be read as struggling. So they perform stability.

Sometimes the performance holds for a while. Sometimes it holds right up to the point the person stops showing up, or quits, or breaks visibly in a way that could have been caught weeks earlier. The manager reads the performance and not the fatigue underneath, because the performance is all that is being shown. By the time the surface cracks, the reading had been wrong for months.

This is not a character problem. It is the same asymmetry that makes smoothness a poor proof of trust, now applied to running on empty. Under fatigue, the flattest voice in the one-on-one is the one to watch. The person who used to ramble about the work and now gives a clean, short answer has hopefully become more efficient, but is more likely just being very careful.

The *Notice* step in Chapter 5 is what catches this. The rhythm forces you to look at each person every week, not just the ones whose signals are easy to read. People performing stability have to keep performing it. A week is a long time to hold a version of yourself that is not quite true.

One specific tell: the answer to *"How are things going?"* that used to carry specifics and is now general. When the specifics drop out, you are usually watching performance.

What to Absorb, What to Surface

The point is not enduring more. It is sorting better. Your job is to know what belongs to you, what belongs to the team, what belongs to the system, and what should not be carried at all.

Some pressure is yours to take.

- **Executive anxiety that would change nothing if the team heard it.** If the VP is nervous about next quarter but the work the team is doing is already the right work, you do not need to pass the nerves down. You need to keep the work steady.

- **Political noise from reorgs and restructures.** Who is now reporting to whom three levels up, whose team got renamed, what budget conversations are happening in rooms you were not invited to. Your team does not need running commentary. They need to know what, if anything, actually changes for them.

- **Unclear priorities you can triangulate yourself.** If you can piece together what leadership actually wants from context, do that work on your side and hand the team a clean version. Do not hand them the ambiguity.

- **Requests from adjacent teams that aren't yours.** Someone asking for a favor that doesn't serve your team's goals is your problem to decline, not your team's problem to absorb.

- **The performance of calm during uncertainty.** Your face and your voice are part of the information environment your team is reading. You are allowed to feel worried. You are not allowed to let worry become the team's mood.

Most managers will absorb anything that can be absorbed, and a few things that cannot. But some pressure is not yours to take. Pretending it is does real damage.

- **Timelines the team cannot meet.** If the date is wrong, say so. Absorbing an impossible timeline by working the team harder is how the team ends up hating the work.

- **Headcount and tooling gaps that are breaking the work.** If the team cannot do what is being asked with what they have, that is a constraint leadership needs to know about. Shielding them from it means they cannot make the tradeoffs only they can make.

- **Decisions that need upstream clarity before anyone can act.** If you are unsure whether you are allowed to do X, asking is cheaper than guessing.

- **Pressure you cannot absorb without lying to the team.** If the only way to keep the pressure off the team is to tell them something that is not true, the pressure is no longer absorbable. It has to go upward.

Shielding, Not Lying

The hardest of those is the last. Shielding is a short-term transfer of cost, where you take the discomfort now so the team can do the work now and the situation resolves itself within a known window. Lying is the same move made permanent. The situation is not going to resolve, the team will find out eventually, and when they do, the trust you spent to shield them is the trust they use to conclude you cannot be trusted.

The line between the two is harder to see in the moment than it is on paper. Most managers do not set out to lie. They delay a conversation because the timing is bad. They soften a piece of news because the team is already stretched. They hope the situation will change before they have to say it out loud. Each of those moves is shielding if the situation does resolve. Each becomes a lie the moment it does not.

If you are not sure which one you are doing, ask yourself what happens if the team finds out later that you knew. If the answer is "they would understand why I held it," you are shielding. If the answer is "they would be angry," you are lying.

Honest shielding has an expiration. You hold the weight, and you keep a clock on it. When the window closes — the reorg announces itself, the timeline slips officially, the decision gets made upstream — you surface what you held, and you explain what you held and why. Shielding is remembered as care. Discovered lying is remembered as betrayal, even when the motive was the same.

Hold People to Their Promises

The same softening shows up inside the team. When people are tired, your willingness to hold the line on commitments they made when the energy was higher gets weaker. Your instinct will be to soften. People are already stretched, the promise is not central to the main work, surely it is kinder to let it slide. That instinct is almost always wrong. What looks like kindness in the moment teaches the team that commitments here are optional. The next time someone makes one, they will hold it lightly, because they have seen the precedent.

Holding people to their own promises is care for the thing they said they wanted to do.

We ran a book club on the team. Each person read a chapter and presented it. The reading mattered, but the point was practicing presentations and running something outside the day job. We rotated who organized each round.

One team member volunteered for a round in which sixteen people had committed to present. Three weeks out, several presenters hadn't started their slides. A week later, same story. The presenters weren't ignoring him; they were busy, and the book club came second to their day jobs.

He couldn't bring himself to push. These people had volunteered their time. Who was he to pressure them?

I coached him through it. They volunteered because they wanted to grow, and they would never have time unless they made it. His job was not to accept the slip; it was to protect the commitment they had made to themselves. Letting it go would teach everyone that commitments here were optional. He was respecting their word, not pressuring them.

He made the calls. The presentations happened on schedule. After that, he stopped treating accountability as confrontation.

Look Back

The hard periods leave lessons only if the team goes back to them. The reviews people skip most often are the ones after the pressure lifts — the project shipped, the reorg settled, the crisis passed. Skip the debrief and the team carries the next hard period with less than the last one could have taught.

The toolkit at the back of the book has an After-Action Review card with the four questions. Three rules make the difference between a debrief that produces learning and a meeting that wastes an hour.

Do it soon. Memory degrades fast; after two weeks you are debriefing a distorted memory, not the thing itself. *Start with your own mistakes.* If the manager cannot name what they got wrong, the team will also stay abstract. *Separate the system from the person.* "The deployment process failed" generates analysis; "you failed at the deployment" closes it. Good debriefs fix the system without shaming the people.

A team with this kind of institutional memory handles the next crisis differently. A team without it repeats the same mistake, and the lesson stays in the manager's head where the team cannot reach it.

Know What the Work Does to You

The Ladder does not only reveal the people you lead. Over time, the work reveals you.

You learn your role — what the moment actually asks of you when the pressure rises. Not the title. Not the job description. Are you the person who clarifies, absorbs, names, shields, escalates, decides? Or are you the person who disappears into activity because activity feels safer than judgment?

You learn your range. Some managers are calm in crisis and avoidant in conflict. Some are generous with development and careless with follow-through. Some can carry executive pressure without passing it down, but cannot sit still when a report is disappointed in them. Range is where your steadiness runs out.

You learn your drive. The work will show you whether you manage from service, ambition, fear, approval, control, or some mixture of all of them. Most managers are not driven by one clean thing; the danger is refusing to see the mix. A manager who needs to be liked will avoid the correction until the silence becomes unfair. A manager who needs to be indispensable will keep decisions routed through themselves and call it support. A manager who needs to be seen as strong will absorb pressure that should have been named.

Then there is your horizon. The job is making you into someone. The question is whether you are watching who that person is. Every hard season leaves a mark, like a little more patience, a little more cynicism, a little more courage, a little more distance. None of it happens all at once. You become the manager you repeatedly practice being.

And eventually, if you stay honest, you learn your fears. The executive you will not challenge. The report you overprotect because you cannot bear to see them disappointed. The high performer you keep overusing because you are afraid the team cannot carry the work without them. The silence you fill because you are afraid of what might come after it. The decision you delay because deciding would make someone unhappy with you.

Reading yourself is the same accuracy you owe the team. The manager who does not know what the work does to them will eventually pass that distortion to the team. Their fear becomes urgency. Their fatigue becomes distance. Their need for approval becomes unclear standards. Their resentment becomes a tone people learn to manage.

You do not need to become endlessly self-aware. You need enough honesty to know when you are no longer seeing clearly. That is part of what you carry.

What the Work Leaves in the Team

The same attention that reveals the manager to themselves leaves a residue in the team. The disciplines you practiced visibly under pressure are the ones the team will reach for the next time the pressure rises, whether you are still there or not. The way you debriefed a miss becomes how they debrief their own. The questions you asked instead of supplying answers become the way they coach each other. The conversations you had about a missed inheritor become how they catch the next one.

That residue is what outlasts the manager. The team's good character is not a memory of you. It is the working habits you helped them practice often enough that those habits became how they work. You do not get to choose which habits form into character. The team takes the disciplines you practiced consistently, not the ones you named in offsite slides. What you skipped is also part of the residue.

The weekly rhythm practiced under good conditions becomes the rhythm that holds when conditions are bad and you are not in the room. That is the longer-arc reason the rhythm matters.

The Weight You Carry

Week by week, you decide what belongs to the team and what does not. You tell the truth without letting despair become the team's weather. You hold people to what they promised when they were stronger, because those commitments belong to them, and you are the one protecting them.

The danger is not that the work gets heavy. It will. The danger is that the weight changes what you see. You start mistaking quiet for alignment, compliance for commitment, your own need for relief for the team's actual capacity. That is when pressure stops being something you carry and becomes something you transmit.

The whole book asks one thing of the manager: to keep seeing clearly. Each chapter teaches a different way of paying attention. This one is about doing all of that while the work is hard and the picture in your head is the first thing under threat.

Under pressure, keep seeing clearly.

Three Ideas to Carry

- **Endurance is not the goal. Accuracy is.** The manager's job is to know what belongs to them, what belongs to the team, and what belongs to the system. Carrying everything quietly is not virtue; it is misallocation.

- **Shielding has an expiration. Lying does not.** The line between the two is whether the team finds out later, and what they conclude about you when they do. If the answer is "they would understand why I held it," you are shielding. If the answer is "they would be angry," you are lying.

- **You are becoming someone the work is making.** Watch who that person is. The picture in your head is the first thing under threat when the pressure rises, and the manager who does not know what the work does to them eventually passes the distortion to the team.

What They Remember

— Annie Dillard

"He listened to me better than I listened to myself."

I am still getting this wrong. When the team is strong, the rhythm feels optional. The weekly rhythm slides. Meetings fill the space it used to hold. I still think I know them. I did, six months ago. The manager is supposed to grow with the team and stay a step ahead of it. A capable team disguises that obligation. They grow. I keep up with the day. The day wins, and the picture of them in my head stays frozen at last quarter.

Most of what I know about this job, I learned because the rhythm taught it to me. Most of what I forget, I forget because the rhythm slipped. The Ladder is a picture you can draw on a napkin. The climb is the twenty-five minutes you have to protect from yourself.

The climb is worth it for what it does on the other side of the desk. The person who is truly seen stops performing and starts thinking. That is why the Truth Ladder matters. Not because deeper knowledge produces better outcomes on a dashboard. But because the person who is truly known stops hiding.

The knowing has a ceiling, and I do not set it alone. On the other side of the desk, the person is still doing the math on what is safe to say. The careful version of them may be the only version I ever see. The job is to behave in ways that let the price of truth fall, and to respect the careful version when it does not.

Management is the temporary custody of people's working lives. You are holding their time, energy, and growth. What you do with that time stays with them. Sit with that long enough and you feel the gap between what you wanted to give and what you actually did.

I am not the leader I want to be. Some weeks, the day still wins. I still confuse yesterday's knowledge with today's truth. But next week, I get another twenty-five minutes. I can protect it. I can ask better. I can listen longer. I can climb again.

That is the job.

In This Chapter

Appendix: Manager's Toolkit

The tools below are drawn from the chapters of this book. They help you do the work this book is about: knowing each person on your team well enough to help them, with outcomes clear enough that the helping reaches them. They are reference cards, not summaries. The chapters have the reasoning.

Working the Toolkit

The Quick Start at the front of the book is the on-ramp if you are starting from zero. The cards below are reference. To use them well, work the five steps in order — then pick one card from the rest each week.

1. **Map each report on the Truth Ladder.** Where are you with each person — role, range, drive, horizon, or fears? *(See: The Truth Ladder.)*

2. **Read for the gradient.** Ask, for each person, where power distorts what you hear. *(See: The Gradient.)*

3. **Restructure your one-on-ones.** Five sections, 25 minutes, employee-led. *(See: One-on-One Structure Card.)*

4. **Run the weekly rhythm.** Ask, Listen, Connect, Notice, Stretch — 8–15 minutes per person. (Chapter 5)

5. **Pick one card from the rest each week.** Recognition, feedback in the moment, a handoff contract, the career conversation guide. Choose what your team needs first.

The Truth Ladder and the practices that climb it.

- **Truth Ladder** — Role → Range → Drive → Horizon → Fears. Five levels of knowing each person. (Chapter 1)
- **The weekly rhythm** — Ask, Listen, Connect, Notice, Stretch. Five directions of attention spread across a month. (Chapter 5)
- **The context frame** — the why, the win, the boundaries, the how. What clear outcomes look like when they reach a person. (Chapter 11)

Manager Self-Assessment

Ten questions drawn from the core practices in this book. There is no score. Answer each one honestly — the ones that give you pause point you at the chapter to revisit.

1. Has every person on my team received specific recognition from me in the past seven days? (Chapter 9)
2. Which of the four patterns am I in with my team overall — ghost, boss, friend, or leader? (Chapter 1)
3. For each person on my team, what level of the Truth Ladder am I at? Where am I stuck? (Chapter 1)
4. Do people bring me problems early, or late? (Chapter 3)
5. When someone disagrees with me, do they say it in the room or only after? (Chapter 2)
6. Where does work consistently slow down when it changes hands on my team? (Chapter 12)
7. Can I name what motivates each person on my team — specifically, not in general? (Chapter 8)
8. In a one-on-one, is my share of the talking closer to 10% or 50%? (Chapter 7)
9. Have I cancelled a one-on-one in the past month? (Chapter 6)
10. Can each person on my team articulate how their work connects to the team's goals? (Chapter 11)

If most feel solid, you are doing the work. If several gave you pause, you know where to focus. Pick one. Start this week.

The Four Patterns

Outcomes crossed with depth of knowing. Where are you with your team overall? (Chapter 1)

- **Ghost** — vague outcomes, surface knowledge.
- **Boss** — clear outcomes, surface knowledge.
- **Friend** — deep knowledge, vague outcomes.
- **Leader** — clear outcomes, deep knowledge.

Move toward the leader.

The Truth Ladder

Five levels of knowing each person. Where are you with each one? (Chapter 1)

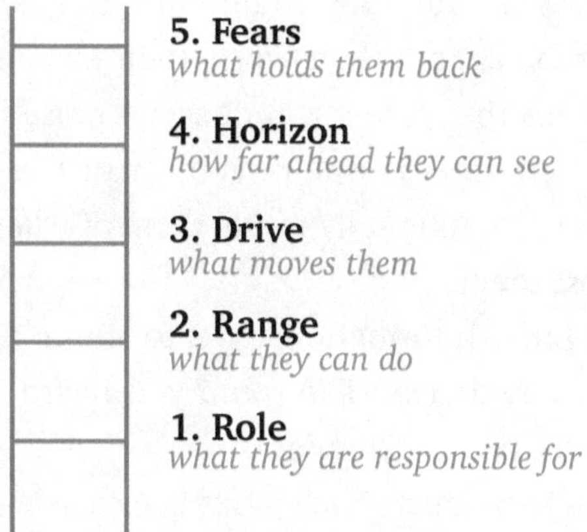

What each rung unlocks:

1. **Role.** You can assign work.
2. **Range.** You can give useful feedback and assign the right work.
3. **Drive.** You can motivate without guessing.
4. **Horizon.** You can develop their career.
5. **Fears.** You can coach through what matters most.

Most managers stop at Level 1. Level 5 is earned through months of trust and listening.

The Gradient

The gradient is the power asymmetry between a manager and a direct report — and what that asymmetry does to honesty. Power changes what your reports tell you: they route what they say through risk, because your opinion shapes their work, their evaluation, their next door. Warmth softens the gradient. It does not erase it. (Chapter 2)

Two clocks. Every one-on-one runs on two: the conversation in front of you, and the running tally inside them of what the last honest thing they said cost them.

The Evidence Line. Information given to you in confidence is not available to you as evidence. The room you heard it in is the only room it is allowed to be in. (Chapter 4)

Five false signals of trust. Each looks like closeness. Each is often something else.

1. **Quick agreement** — the fastest exit from a conversation with weight.
2. **Warmth** — friendliness that costs nothing to give.
3. **A hard story** — one door opened, the rest still closed.
4. **Gratitude** — often the form caution takes when the downside is severe.
5. **Polished articulacy** — fluency that mirrors your language back at you.

What lowers the cost of truth. Ask less invasive questions. Watch behavior more than declarations. Treat volunteered vulnerability carefully — disclosure is a data point, not a verdict. Wait two seconds before responding to a hard thing.

Self-check. Do my reports revise my thinking, or mostly receive it? Bring half-formed problems, or only polished updates? Tell me my framing is wrong when it is? Ask for help before the miss, or only after? Set boundaries without a long justification? Disagree in the room, or only afterwards?

Handoff Contract Template

Use this the next time a handoff between two people on your team is going wrong. Put them in a room together and ask them to fill it in, in their own words. Do not write it for them. (Chapter 12)

Handoff: *[person A, role]* → *[person B, role]*

Scope: *(one sentence describing what kind of work crosses this boundary)*

1. What is "done"?

What specifically has to be complete on A's side before the handoff? What does "finished" mean? List the artifacts, files, documents, or states that must exist.

2. What assumptions were made?

What does A believe to be true when they decide what to decide? What context shapes the work that might not be obvious to B?

3. What quality bar was used?

Rough draft meant to provoke discussion? Decision-ready recommendation? Something ready to ship? Name the bar and agree on it.

4. What risks remain?

What still looks uncertain, fragile, or under-tested? What does A wish they had more time for? What is going to break first?

5. Who owns the next move?

After the handoff, who is responsible for the next action? When is it expected? What is B empowered to decide without checking back?

How we raise it when the contract is broken:

What does A say to B, or B say to A, when the last handoff fell short? Write the opening sentence here. *"The last handoff was missing X. Can we fix it before the next one?"* is the kind of sentence that has to feel safe to say.

Revisit this document at the first signs of renewed friction. The contract exists to outlive the conversation that created it.

Three Kinds of Conversation

Every one-on-one contains three. After every meeting, ask which one you skipped. (Chapter 6)

- **Outcome** — priorities, blockers, next steps. The least risky conversation.
- **Person** — how are you, really? Where Levels 3 and 4 of the Ladder open.
- **Growth** — where do you want to be, and what is the gap? Horizon work.

Default to outcome and the rest of the system cannot load.

One-on-One Structure Card

Five sections, 25 minutes, every week. The employee sets the agenda. (Chapter 6)

1. **Accomplishments** (5 min) — What went well this week? What are you proud of?
2. **Blocked items** (5–10 min) — Where are you stuck? What do you need from me?
3. **Next week** (5 min) — What are your top priorities? Are we aligned?
4. **Areas to develop** (5 min) — What skill are you working on? How is it going?
5. **Quarterly goals** (as needed) — Where do we stand against our targets?

When they bring you a problem, resist solving it. Ask instead:

- What have you considered so far?
- What's the risk you're most worried about?
- What would you do if you had to decide right now?
- What would need to be true for this plan to fail?

End every meeting with something forward-looking. "Based on what you just told me, I think you're heading in the right direction on ___."

The 25/50 Rule

Schedule meetings for 25 or 50 minutes instead of 30 or 60. Start on time and end early on purpose.

Back-to-back calls create a cascade where every meeting starts with someone still processing the last one. They join physically present but mentally elsewhere. A five-minute gap lets people stand up, refill coffee, glance at the next agenda, or just let their brain catch up. The meeting itself gets tighter, because when you know the clock stops at 25, you skip the slow warmup and get to the point.

One detail that matters: start on time and end at minute 25 or minute 50. Do not start at :05 or :10 to "give people a buffer." The discipline is structural — end early on purpose. If you start five minutes late, the meeting still runs to the hour, because there is no structural reason to stop.

Work expands to fill the time available for its completion[1] — shrink the container and the work shrinks with it.

Set your calendar defaults to 25 and 50 minutes. For more on this practice, see 2550.org.[2]

Decision Meeting: Four Questions

For a group evaluating an idea together, run through these in order. No one attacks, no one defends; everyone is thinking from the same angle at the same time. (Chapter 11)

1. **Benefit — What do we gain?** The upside and the beneficiaries. Start here so the idea gets a fair hearing before the conversation turns critical.

2. **Enablers — Who do we need?** Input, approval, or expertise required. A long list is a signal — simplify the idea or expect a slower path.

3. **Blockers — What is blocking us?** Systemic obstacles. Cost, time, technical debt, regulatory constraints — and the ongoing weight of success: operations, maintenance, on-call, hiring.

4. **Risk — What if we fail?** Blast radius and what is lost if it does not work.

Work through all four together, taking notes as you go. If the picture is clear, decide. If the idea needs more research, a cost estimate, or a conversation with another team, defer — that is discipline, not indecision. Either way, the person who proposed the idea does not leave the room feeling attacked. The team examined the idea, not the person.

The Inheritors Question

Before the work starts, ask: *who inherits this?* Not who approved it. Who lives with it after delivery, two years from now, at 3am when it breaks. (Chapter 13)

The owner page. Write it before scoping. Two columns: the four parts of the context frame, and the owner of each.

- **Why** — the sponsor; whoever needs the outcome.
- **Win** — whoever defines what success looks like.
- **Boundaries** — break this one out by domain: runtime to operations, compliance to legal or security, downstream contracts to consuming teams.
- **How** — the team.

A blank cell tells you where the next conversation is. A cell with two names tells you where the next disagreement will come from.

Inheritors who most often get missed:

- **Operators** — run the system day to day; hold the boundaries of operational reality.
- **Supporters** — get paged when it fails; hold the boundaries of failure cost.
- **Maintainers** — inherit the work two years from now; hold the boundaries of sustainability.
- **Consumers** — downstream teams whose own work depends on this one's output; hold contract-shaped boundaries.
- **Reviewers** — compliance, legal, security, procurement; hold the boundaries the project cannot negotiate.

None of them hide. They get missed because the project's center of gravity is somewhere else, and their rooms are further from it than the requester's.

If you missed one. Pull the project back to the four parts. Write the page now. Then sit with the inheritor and lead with what you got wrong about their world, not their constraint. The retrofit fixes the project; the relationship is a slower repair.

After-Action Review

After every project completion, every product launch, every major client engagement, and every quarter, gather the team and run the four questions. The format is borrowed from the U.S. Army. (Chapter 15)

1. **What did we intend to achieve?**
2. **What actually happened?**
3. **Why did it happen?**
4. **What do we change?**

Start with your own mistakes: "Here's what I got wrong in how I scoped this project." If the manager can admit error without consequence, everyone else can too.

Three rules make the difference between a debrief that produces learning and a meeting that wastes an hour.

Do it immediately. Memory degrades fast. If you wait two weeks to run a retrospective, you are debriefing a distorted memory of what happened, not what actually happened.

Separate identity from behavior. "The deployment process failed" is a systemic observation. "You failed at the deployment" is a personal attack. The first generates analysis, the second defensiveness. All feedback in a debrief should be directed at the system, the process, or the decision, never at the person.

End with commitments. A debrief that produces insights but no action items is a well-documented failure. Every debrief should conclude with specific, assigned changes. "Next time, we will test the integration environment 48 hours before launch, and Sarah will own that checkpoint." Without commitments, the same mistakes repeat.

Career Conversation Guide

Twice a year, separate from your regular one-on-one. This is forward-looking and driven by the employee's aspirations. (Chapter 10)

Before the conversation:

- What has this person accomplished since our last career conversation?
- Where are they growing? Where are they stuck?
- What opportunities could I create or connect them to?
- The first answer is usually the approved one. Treat it as the surface; the truer version comes after a few rounds without cost.

Five questions to ask:

1. Where do you want to be in two to three years?
2. What skills do you need to develop to get there?
3. What experiences would stretch you?
4. What's getting in the way right now?
5. How can I help?

After the conversation:

Write down one commitment: "By [date], I will help [name] with [specific action]." Follow up in your regular one-on-ones. If you ask about their career twice a year and do nothing in between, you have trained them to stop answering honestly.

Recognition Quick Reference

Three sentences, thirty seconds, at least once a week per person. (Chapter 9)

The structure:

1. **What they did.** Name the specific action. Not "great work" — the actual thing.
2. **Why it mattered.** Connect it to a result, a customer, a teammate, or a goal.
3. **What it says about them.** Name the skill or quality it demonstrated.

Example: "The way you handled the client escalation on Tuesday kept the whole situation from spiraling. That saved the account and probably saved us the weekend. That's the kind of judgment I want the whole team to learn from."

Self-check — is your recognition:

- *Specific* — naming what they did and why it mattered, not "great job"?
- *Timely* — delivered close to the moment, not saved for review season?
- *Calibrated* — public or private, written or spoken, the way this person prefers?
- *Equitable* — reaching everyone, not just the loudest or most visible?
- *Consistent* — a weekly rhythm, not an occasional burst?

Audit the last 30 days. Write down everyone you named in front of others or in writing, and what you said about them. If the same names recur and others never appear, the gap is structural, not anecdotal.

Mistakes that kill recognition:

- Inconsistency. Enthusiastic for two weeks, silent for three months.

- Coupling praise with criticism. "Great work, but next time..." Save the coaching for a separate conversation.
- Delegating it to a platform. Technology can amplify recognition. It cannot replace you saying it.

Feedback in the Moment

When you see something that needs to be said, say it while the moment is still warm. Don't save it for a scheduled meeting. Don't generalize. (Chapter 3)

Three moves:

1. **What you saw.** Describe the specific behavior. "In the design review this morning, you spoke over Maya twice when she was presenting her approach." Stay on the action, not the person.

2. **What it did.** Name the impact. "After the second time, she stopped contributing. The team lost her input on the trade-offs we needed to evaluate." Without impact, an observation is just surveillance.

3. **What you're curious about.** Ask, don't prescribe. "What was going on for you in that moment?" Then listen.

Three conditions:

- *Proximity* — close to the moment, not days or weeks later.
- *Specificity* — the actual behavior, not a pattern you have been silently accumulating.
- *Curiosity* — a genuine question about their side, not a rhetorical one.

Common mistakes:

- Waiting until the one-on-one. The moment has cooled. It now sounds like a verdict.
- Staying vague. "You need to be more collaborative" gives them nothing to act on.
- Skipping the question. Without it, you are delivering a lecture, not starting a conversation.
- Softening it into nothing. "I'm sure you didn't mean it, but..." tells them you don't believe what you're about to say.

Receiving feedback:

The same structure works in reverse. When someone gives you feedback: listen, don't defend, summarize what you heard, and thank them. If you give direct feedback but can't receive it, people will stop telling you what you need to hear.

Damaging Boss Protocol

Most upward relationships can be worked with using the practices in Chapter 14. A few cannot. This card is for the case where the person above you is the source of the harm: a quiet pattern of being diminished in rooms you are not in, and used as a shield when things go wrong. The managing-up practices will not save a relationship like this. They may buy time; they will not fix a person who is not interested in being a good manager.

What counts as damaging. A pattern across months, with the same direction of harm, not a single bad day.

- **Credit moved.** Your work, your ideas, your write-ups come back in their voice without attribution.
- **Blame placed.** You are named as the cause of problems you flagged in writing and could not have prevented.
- **Commitments broken in the same direction.** Follow-through fails consistently on the things that would cost them — the promotion case, the headcount ask, the cover with the VP.
- **Information withheld strategically.** You find out late about decisions that affect your team, and late is convenient for them.
- **Public diminishment.** Small undercuts in meetings: the tone correction, the visible skepticism, the dismissive reframe of what you said.

Four moves. Not parallel choices. They run in sequence and in parallel, each with its own trigger.

1. **Document — start now.** Trigger: the first time you notice the pattern. Keep a private, contemporaneous log: date, what happened, an artifact or witness. Outside company systems. The log is insurance against your own memory, and against the version of events the organization may later be told.

2. **Shield the team — while you stay.** Trigger: as soon as the weather above could reach them. Do not pass blame down. Do not relay commitments you do not trust as facts. Do not broadcast your boss's dysfunction. Absorb what can be absorbed; leave the temperature out of debriefs.

3. **Escalate patterns, not incidents.** Trigger: a documented pattern across multiple incidents and several weeks, *and* direct feedback to the person with a reasonable window for change, *and* the behavior has continued or worsened. Three paths: skip-level (your boss's boss) for a documented pattern; HR or employee relations for harassment, retaliation, discrimination, or legal exposure; external counsel if the pattern includes credible retaliation or you are being set up for a performance action that does not match the record. Accelerated trigger: behavior crossing into harassment, retaliation, discrimination, or legal exposure — the feedback precondition does not apply. Go straight to HR or external counsel.

4. **Set a decision deadline.** Trigger: the cost of staying — in health, confidence, time outside work, the version of yourself you are becoming — has begun to exceed the specific reasons to stay. Write down, privately, the condition or the date that would make you leave. Then honor it. The slow boil is what people lose themselves to. Sunk cost is not an argument for more months. Interview even when you do not want to leave; the information changes how you read the situation.

A note on the math. Staying costs more than the hours. Some of that is recoverable. Some is not. Reasons to stay are usually specific: a milestone that changes your options, a market that is bad enough to hold you, a team that needs you through a particular moment. Those are legitimate. Sunk cost is not. Leaving a manager who diminishes you to protect themselves is a form of self-respect, not a failure of resilience.

Notes

Introduction

1. Chartered Management Institute (2023), *Better Managers: The Business Case for Investing in Management and Leadership Development*: 82% of those entering management had not received proper training. Gallup (2025), *State of the Global Workplace*: only 30% of front-line supervisors obtained their roles based on supervisory skills; 65% were promoted based on performance or tenure.

Chapter 1: The Truth Ladder

1. Harter, J.K. et al. (2024). "Gallup Q12 Meta-Analysis Report." Gallup. — Examining 100,000+ teams across decades of data. Top-quartile teams outperform bottom-quartile teams by roughly a fifth in profitability and sales productivity, and by roughly half the turnover in retention. Published as a Gallup technical report, not in a peer-reviewed journal; the peer-reviewed foundation is Harter, Schmidt & Hayes (2002) in *JAP*.

2. Harter, J.K., Schmidt, F.L., Asplund, J.W., Killham, E.A. & Agrawal, S. (2010). "Causal Impact of Employee Work Perceptions on the Bottom Line of Organizations." *Perspectives on Psychological Science*, 5(4), 378–389. Longitudinal study of 2,178 business units in 10 organizations confirming that engagement causally precedes business-unit performance.

3. Gallup (2017). "The No. 1 Employee Benefit That No One's Talking About." — One in two employees have left a job to get away from a manager.

4. Buckingham, M. & Coffman, C. (1999). *First, Break All the Rules: What the World's Greatest Managers Do Differently*. Simon & Schuster. The book's core finding, drawn from Gallup interviews with over 80,000 managers, was that the strongest managers tailored their approach to the individual rather than treating reports interchangeably.

5. Edmondson, A. (1999). Psychological Safety and Learning Behavior in Work Teams. *Administrative Science Quarterly*.

Chapter 3: Trust Before Truth

1. Brown, B. (2018). *Dare to Lead: Brave Work. Tough Conversations. Whole Hearts.* Random House. Brown frames going first as a vulnerability discipline — the courage to show up before knowing how it will be received. The framing here overlaps and differs: under the gradient, going first is also a price move. The person with more power pays the cost of disclosure first so the report can read what the cost might be for them.

2. Mayer, R. C., Davis, J. H., & Schoorman, F. D. (1995). "An Integrative Model of Organizational Trust." *Academy of Management Review*, 20(3), 709–734.

3. Simons, T. (2002). Behavioral Integrity: The Perceived Alignment Between Managers' Words and Deeds as a Research Focus. *Organization Science*, 13(1), 18–35.

4. Kim, P.H., Ferrin, D.L., Cooper, C.D. & Dirks, K.T. (2004). "Removing the Shadow of Suspicion: The Effects of Apology Versus Denial for Repairing Competence- Versus Integrity-Based Trust Violations." *Journal of Applied Psychology*, 89(1), 104–118. The study finds that apology is more effective than denial for competence-based violations; for integrity-based violations, the dynamics are more complex. In management practice, taking full responsibility remains the strongest first step when the manager knows they were at fault.

Chapter 6: Three Kinds of Conversation

1. Rogelberg, S.G. (2024). *Glad We Met: The Art and Science of 1:1 Meetings.* Oxford University Press. Based on surveys of thousands of managers and employees, managers consistently rate the quality and effectiveness of their one-on-ones significantly higher than the employees in those same meetings do.

2. Sprecher, S. et al. (2013). "Taking turns: Reciprocal self-disclosure promotes liking in initial interactions." *Journal of Experimental Social Psychology*. Reciprocal disclosure between strangers in initial interactions increased affection, connection, perceived similarity, and enjoyment.

3. Minson, J. et al. "Personal Narratives Build Trust Across Ideological Divides." *Harvard Kennedy School.* "Data and facts can only take the conversation so far."

4. Rogelberg, S.G. (2022). "Make the Most of Your One-on-One Meetings." *Harvard Business Review*, November–December 2022. Based on a global survey of 1,000 knowledge workers, a U.S. survey of 250 one-on-one participants and leaders, and interviews with nearly 50 Fortune 100 leaders. Weekly meetings of 20–30 minutes correlated with the highest engagement levels at every level. The cadence is correlated with engagement, not proven to cause it; the practical takeaway is that weekly twenty-to-thirty-minute meetings are where the strongest engagement consistently shows up. See also Rogelberg, S.G. (2024). *Glad We Met: The Art and Science of 1:1 Meetings.* Oxford University Press.

5. Gallup (2024). "The One Great Manager Habit That Drives Employee Engagement." *Gallup Workplace.* Only 15% of employees without routine manager check-ins are engaged; with regular, meaningful conversations, engagement rises nearly threefold. The relationship is correlational; routine check-ins co-occur with other practices of attentive management, and the multiplier should be read as engagement moving with manager rhythm rather than caused by it alone.

Chapter 7: Listen for What Wasn't Said

1. Zenger, J. & Folkman, J. (2016). "What Great Listeners Actually Do." *Harvard Business Review*, July 2016. Analysis of 3,492 participants: self-assessment of listening parallels driving skills. The best listeners amplify and clarify ideas through questions and engagement rather than absorbing them passively.

2. Kruger, J. & Dunning, D. (1999). "Unskilled and Unaware of It: How Difficulties in Recognizing One's Own Incompetence Lead to Inflated Self-Assessments." *Journal of Personality and Social Psychology*, 77(6), 1121–1134. Participants scoring in the 12th percentile estimated performance at the 62nd percentile.

3. Rogers, C.R. & Farson, R.E. (1957). *Active Listening.* "Sensitive listening is a most effective agent for individual personality change and group development."

4. Rogers, C.R. & Farson, R.E. (1957). "It requires that we get inside the speaker, that we grasp, from his point of view, just what it is he is communicating to us."

5. Bregman, P. (2012). "If You Want People to Listen, Stop Talking." *Harvard Business Review*, May 2012. "Silence is a greatly underestimated source of power."

6. Institute of Coaching, McLean Hospital / Harvard Medical School (2019). *Coaching in Practice.* "There is no silence. The coachee is having an internal conversation with themselves."

7. Schifrin, D. (2024). "Listen to summarize the problem, not to solve it." Harvard Business Review.

Chapter 9: Proof That You Noticed

1. Gallup & Workhuman (2024). *Unleashing the Human Element at Work: Transforming Workplaces Through Recognition.* Longitudinal study of nearly 3,500 employees (2022–2024): well-recognized employees were 45% less likely to have turned over after two years. Only 32% strongly agree they receive fair and equitable recognition, with disparities across racial groups.

2. Kohn, A. (1993). *Punished by Rewards.* Houghton Mifflin. For the empirical record, Deci, E.L., Koestner, R., & Ryan, R.M. (1999). "A meta-analytic review of experiments examining the effects of extrinsic rewards on intrinsic motivation." *Psychological Bulletin*, 125(6), 627–668: tangible contingent rewards reduce intrinsic motivation; verbal informational feedback does not, and can enhance it.

3. Gallup. "Q12 Employee Engagement Survey." The Q12 measures whether employees feel their opinions count, as a foundational engagement driver alongside recognition.

4. Morrison, E.W. (2014). "Employee Voice and Silence." *Annual Review of Organizational Psychology and Organizational Behavior*, 1, 173–197. Employees speak up roughly 24% more often when they believe managers act on input.

5. Gallup & Workhuman (2022). *Unleashing the Human Element at Work.* Most memorable recognition sources: direct manager (28%), high-level leader or CEO (24%), manager's manager (12%). 64% of employees prefer a mix of public and private recognition.

6. SHRM & Globoforce (2018). *Using Recognition and Other Workplace Efforts to Engage Employees.* Companies with peer-to-peer recognition programs saw significant improvements in engagement, customer satisfaction, and retention.

Chapter 10: Give Them the Work That Grows Them

1. Kaye, B. & Giulioni, J.W. (2019). *Help Them Grow or Watch Them Go*, 2nd ed. Berrett-Koehler. Performance reviews are evaluative and compensation-linked; career conversations require a separate, exploratory space.

2. Kaye, B. & Giulioni, J.W. (2019). *Help Them Grow or Watch Them Go*, 2nd ed. Berrett-Koehler. Three types of career conversations — hindsight, foresight, and insight —

integrated into regular one-on-ones. "Career development is the single most powerful tool managers have for driving retention, engagement, productivity, and results."

3. Gallup (2024). Frequent, meaningful career conversations are among the strongest predictors of employee engagement.

4. Hewlett, S.A. (2013). *Forget a Mentor, Find a Sponsor: The New Way to Fast-Track Your Career.* Harvard Business Review Press. "Mentors advise; sponsors act." Professionals with sponsors were 23% more likely to be satisfied with their rate of advancement than unsponsored peers; for professionals of color, the effect was even larger, at 65%.

5. Dragoni, L. et al. (2009). "Understanding Managerial Development: Integrating Developmental Assignments, Learning Orientation, and Access to Developmental Opportunities." *Academy of Management Journal*, 52(4), 731–743. See also Korn Ferry (2015), *Real World Leadership* survey: stretch assignments ranked as the most valuable developmental experience.

6. Vygotsky, L.S. (1978). *Mind in Society: The Development of Higher Psychological Processes.* Harvard University Press. The zone of proximal development describes the gap between what a learner can do unaided and what they can achieve with guidance or support.

7. Kampkötter, P., Harbring, C. & Hejny, M. (2018). "Job Rotation and Employee Performance: Evidence from a Longitudinal Study in the Financial Services Industry." *International Journal of Human Resource Management*, 29(10), 1709–1739. Longitudinal study of 280,000+ employees found positive effects of job rotations on performance and satisfaction.

8. Deloitte (2019). *Leading the Social Enterprise: Reinvent with a Human Focus.* Deloitte Global Human Capital Trends. Survey data on rotation programs (skills, productivity, cross-department collaboration). 76% of respondents rated internal mobility as important; only 32% believed employees had opportunities to move. The largest barriers: 49% cited the lack of processes to identify and move employees, 46% said managers actively resisted internal mobility.

Chapter 11: The Context Frame

1. Kaplan, R. S., & Norton, D. P. "Making Your Strategy Work on the Frontline." *Harvard Business Review*, June 2010.

2. The intent-vs.-orders framing is David Marquet's; see *Turn the Ship Around!* (Portfolio, 2012), where he develops it as the alternative to a permission-based command structure.

Chapter 13: The Inheritors

1. Python and TypeScript are different programming languages, each with its own runtime, tooling, and operational ecosystem. A team set up to operate one inherits very little from a team set up to operate the other.

Chapter 15: Carry the Weight

1. Amabile, T. & Kramer, S. (2011). *The Progress Principle: Using Small Wins to Ignite Joy, Engagement, and Creativity at Work.* Harvard Business Review Press. Based on analysis of nearly 12,000 diary entries from 238 employees across 7 companies. See also Amabile, T. & Kramer, S. (2011). "The Power of Small Wins." *Harvard Business Review,* May 2011.

Appendix: Manager's Toolkit

1. Parkinson, C. N. (1955). "Parkinson's Law." *The Economist,* November 19, 1955.

2. The 25/50 meeting standard. See for implementation guidance and the case for shorter default meeting lengths.

Index

Colophon

A close friend of mine, Baris, and I used to visit Elit Kitabevi in Taksim. This bookstore carried English-language technical books, which were expensive for college students, but it was our best source. I was drawn to the fonts, layouts, graphics, and chapter titles as much as the content like Unix and networking. I always wanted to know how the physical object was made. I enjoyed every part of making it: picking the body font, drawing the verso layouts, choosing a cover. A small homage, decades later, to the books I used to pick up at Elit Kitabevi, which no longer exists.

For the geeks: I wrote the book in Markdown and built two Python scripts that feed a Makefile pipeline, one path to LaTeX and PDF, one to EPUB from the same sources. The print edition is set in Bitstream Charter at 11pt with Montserrat semibold headings; the "In This Chapter" verso pages are drawn with TikZ. Nano Banana drew the chapter cartoons. I designed the cover in Sketch (more than 60 iterations) and picked the one that won the family vote. My daughter has led her school yearbook for years, so I tell myself the design committee was credentialed.

www.ingramcontent.com/pod-product-compliance
Lightning Source LLC
Chambersburg PA
CBHW020335180726
47991CB00020B/1707